**Richard Williams** was the ch[...] from 1995 to 2012, having pr[...] and the *Independent*. He was th[...] *The Old Grey Whistle Test* and [...] Berlin Jazz Festival from 2015–[...] are *The Death of Ayrton Senna* (19[...], *Racers* (1997), *Enzo Ferrari: A Life* (2002) and *The Last Road Race* (2004) and *A Race with Love and Death* (2020).

## Praise for *The Boy*

'He [Williams] writes skillfully for petrolheads but also those of us whose delight is in the quirky details ... Call it an appreciation of what makes a sporting hero. This book would certainly be the starting point for any screenplay in affectionately setting out why Moss, the racer, was so revered.' **Matt Dickinson,** *The Times*

'Williams's fast-paced and affectionate biography ... captures the bold, engaging spirit of one of Britain's best-loved sporting heroes ... [he] seems incapable of writing a dull sentence about these now legendary racing cars.' **Justin Marozzi,** *Sunday Times*

'Incredibly good value for money. A fine introduction to both a bygone era and one of motorsport's greatest figures.' **Kevin Turner,** *Autosport*

'*The Boy* is not a conventional biography ... it offers 60 short chapters, each focusing on one incident, one person, one car or one aspect of Moss's personality. This proves to be a fresh way of telling a story that's been told many times before ... We are in very safe hands with Richard Williams ... [he] is, as ever, great at juggling the big picture and the tiny detail.' **Colin Overland,** *Car*

'[A] sympathetic, exhaustive anatomy of an international sporting hero, part-time playboy and ultimate family man.' **Patrick Skene Catling,** *Spectator*

# The Boy

## STIRLING MOSS:
## A LIFE IN 60 LAPS

## Richard Williams

**SIMON &
SCHUSTER**

London · New York · Sydney · Toronto · New Delhi

First published in Great Britain by Simon & Schuster UK Ltd, 2021
This edition published in Great Britain by Simon & Schuster UK Ltd, 2022

1 3 5 7 9 10 8 6 4 2

Simon & Schuster UK Ltd
1st Floor
222 Gray's Inn Road
London WC1X 8HB

www.simonandschuster.co.uk
www.simonandschuster.com.au
www.simonandschuster.co.in

Simon & Schuster Australia, Sydney
Simon & Schuster India, New Delhi

A CIP catalogue record for this book
is available from the British Library

Paperback ISBN: 978-1-4711-9847-2
eBook ISBN: 978-1-4711-9846-5

Typeset in Bembo by M Rules
Printed and bound by CPI Group (UK) Ltd, Croydon, CR0 4YY

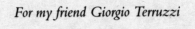

*For my friend Giorgio Terruzzi*

'An automobile race in which Stirling Moss drives a car can have one of two endings. Either Moss wins, or Moss breaks down and someone else wins'

—ALFRED WRIGHT,
*Sports Illustrated*, 1959

# CONTENTS

# CHAPTER 1

# THE LAST TROPHY

Shepherd Market is a small village in the centre of London, on the edge of Mayfair, bounded by Curzon Street to the north and Piccadilly to the south, where for a couple of centuries the signs of discreet wealth and loose morals have happily co-existed. On a summer's day in 2017 I walked up one of its narrow streets with a bag containing a silver statuette, about 18 inches tall: the figure of a racing driver from a bygone era, in helmet and overalls, goggles slung round his neck. I was on my way to deliver it to the house of the man on whom it had been modelled and who, long ago, was known to the newspapers and their readers as 'The Boy'.

A week earlier I'd been due to accompany Sir Stirling Moss and his wife, Lady Susie, on a trip back to Pescara, halfway down Italy's Adriatic coast, for the sixtieth anniversary celebration of a famous victory. The race in 1957 had fascinated me ever since, barely ten years old, I read a report of it in my father's daily newspaper. This was a world championship Grand Prix thrust into the calendar at the last minute, run over a 16-mile course on public roads, from a seaside resort up into the villages in the foothills of the Abruzzi mountains and back again. Moss drove a Vanwall, a British car, beating the powerful Italian teams on their own patch for the first time. Later I'd written a book about it, filled with stories and memories – including his – from a vanished age. After it was published, I was invited to Pescara to take part in a film about the history of racing in the city; now I'd been asked to return for the anniversary, accompanying the guests of honour.

Sadly, Stirling couldn't make the trip. Six months earlier he'd been taken ill on the way home from visiting Australia. What seemed at first like a straightforward respiratory infection had worsened and turned into something else. After several weeks in a Singapore hospital, he'd been brought back to London by a specially chartered medical aircraft. Now he was at home, receiving permanent twenty-four-hour nursing care. He was eighty-seven years old and, as it turned out, he would never be seen in public again.

I was asked to go to Pescara anyway, suddenly promoted to stand in for a legend whose face was on the posters, the programmes, the VIP passes and the labels on the bottles of red wine produced in celebration by a local vineyard. Sadly, he missed out on the sort of reception normally accorded to royalty during a series of lunches, dinners and parades of old sports and racing cars – Maseratis, OSCAs, Alfas, Fiats – through the town and up into the hills, watched by delighted locals and holidaymakers. That welcome came my way instead, including a room at an elegant beachfront hotel, the Esplanade, where one could easily imagine the likes of Moss and his fellow drivers, the generation of Fangio, Hawthorn, Castellotti and Collins, sitting together in the bar on the night before a race. The disappointment at the absence of 'Sir Moss', a man whose reputation in Italy had been established in the days when he was still a teenage prodigy, was intense and widespread, although the organisers were more than generous to his designated substitute.

During the farewell ceremony I was handed the specially commissioned statuette that was to have been presented to him as a permanent keepsake, and asked to take it back to London for him, along with a commemorative plaque and a couple of bottles of the special wine. Then I was shown to the car which had picked me up in Rome two days earlier and in which I was now to be driven back through the mountains to catch a direct flight home to London.

During that four-hour journey across the centre of Italy, I couldn't help reflecting that this was part of the route on which he had won one of his greatest triumphs: the epic Mille Miglia of 1955, thundering to victory in his silver Mercedes over unprotected public roads and through remote villages. Although some of them had since been smoothed out and bypassed, the scenery was still formidable in its remoteness. By the time he reached the Rome control, halfway around the thousand-mile course, he had a lead of seventy-five seconds and was about to defy an old maxim: 'He who leads at Rome will never win the Mille Miglia.'

When I rang the bell at his house, a nurse came to the door. Susie sent her apologies. My visit coincided with a moment when she couldn't leave his bedside. I handed over the trophy and walked away as the door closed on a house full of the memories of his 212 victories from 529 races between 1947 and 1962: the cups and shields, the models of his cars, the diaries recording the events of a racing career, the carefully compiled scrapbooks, and the bent steering wheels from his two biggest crashes, at Spa in 1960 and Goodwood in 1962, mounted and hung on the walls like stags' heads, symbols of his courage in the face of danger. Now one more object had been added to the gallery. I had taken the Boy his last trophy.

# CHAPTER 2

# UNSPOILT

'Heroes were in short supply in 1947,' a Derbyshire doctor wrote in a letter to the *Guardian* during the coronavirus spring of 2020, commenting on a nostalgic article about a season illuminated by the exploits of the cricketer Denis Compton, a dashing figure whose endless flow of runs kept the nation enthralled. As the long years of war began to recede, sport in Britain was getting moving again. Compton and the mesmerising footballer Stanley Matthews were in their pomp, playing to packed houses after picking up the threads of careers that had begun in the 1930s. But Stirling Moss was a fresh face.

The Boy made his competition debut on 2 March 1947 in the Harrow Car Club Trial. He was seventeen years old, his shock of dark hair uncovered as he took the wheel of a BMW 328, a strikingly handsome two-seater sports car. Before the war, this had been a potent machine. Its two-litre straight-six engine had been powerful enough to carry it to a class win in the 1938 Mille Miglia. The car Stirling drove was a right-hand-drive model acquired by his father from a fellow dentist and amateur racer.

In the late 1930s, German racing cars had become unbeatable. Curiously, only a year or two after the end of the war, there was no stigma attached to them among most British car enthusiasts, even though their manufacturers had also made engines for the Messerschmitts and Focke-Wulfs that did battle with the RAF's Spitfires and Hurricanes – an attitude of reconciliation that would be underlined when Moss joined the Mercedes-Benz team a few years later. Now, in his BMW, Stirling won something called the Cullen Cup, which happened to have been donated by his mother.

Compton had just finished punishing the South African bowling with a double century in the second Test, with thousands unable to get into a packed, sun-baked Lord's, when Stirling entered the BMW in his third event. The Junior Car Club rally in Eastbourne included various forms of test – among them parking, steering and acceleration – on the resort's seafront promenade. He was named first in class.

Soon, while still in his teens, he would be winning trophies from Goodwood to Lake Garda and an eager nation would be applauding a prodigy. At twenty, he was presented to the King and Queen before the British Grand Prix. Too young to have served in and been scarred by the war, he was exhibiting the combination of skill, courage and panache celebrated in the generation that had fought in the air and on land and sea. Their youth had been stolen; his was new and unspoilt.

He was the first of his contemporaries to stir the emotions, taking on the continentals in a very modern sport, flying the flag for a country in recovery – material and spiritual – from the damage of war. He was a prodigy whose skills and energy held out the promise of a glorious future. Less obviously to his early fans, he was already taking a professional approach to the job of driving racing cars – and of turning himself into a public figure. 'I was the first professional in England since the war,' he said, 'and the reason that I wanted to become professional was that I couldn't afford to race all the time without making enough money.'

But the romantic image was the one that prevailed. The public saw a young man who loved to fight, often from the underdog's position. Once cast, the spell was never broken. And if he sometimes seemed obsessively restless, even exhaustingly hyperactive, it was explained by his motto: 'Movement is tranquillity'.

His popularity made him almost ubiquitous. It was Moss, rather than others with prominent roles in the rise of Britain in the post-war world of international motor racing, who was chosen for the cover of the men's interest magazine *Lilliput* in the summer of 1951, at the age of twenty-one, and who was regularly featured in the *Eagle*, a comic for middle-class boys, alongside others – like Compton, Matthews and the cyclist Reg Harris – who acted as one-man emblems of their sport. When the *Eagle*'s cartoon detective Harris Tweed became entangled in a plot involving motor racing, the fictional driver was named 'Merling Stoss'. In 1958, Peter Ustinov would affectionately parody him as 'Girling Foss' in his satirical recording *The Grand Prix of Gibraltar*.

He was the first racing driver to be the subject of *This Is Your Life*, to be interviewed on *Face to Face*, and, in 1956, to become a guest on BBC Radio's *Desert Island Discs*. (His choices – clearly those of a man who liked a smooch – were Dave King's 'Memories Are Made of This', 'The Charleston' by the Joe Daniels Jazz Group, Nat King Cole's 'Unforgettable', 'You Talk Jus' Like My Maw' from the soundtrack of the musical *Carmen Jones*, Frank Sinatra's 'The Tender Trap', Lorrae Desmond's 'Hold My Hand' from the film *Susan Slept Here*, Glenn Miller's 'A String of Pearls' and Eartha Kitt's 'Let's Do It'.) Eventually he became the only racing driver in history whose manager, mechanic and personal secretary all published memoirs of their time with him.

His emergence had been perfectly timed. As Britain shook off the memories of wartime austerity and rationing came to an end, the nation sought figures who could become emblematic of a revived optimism. Following the death of George VI in 1952, a new Elizabethan age was declared; to celebrate the coronation of the young Queen, a British-led expedition planted a Union Flag on the summit of Everest. A year later, on a cinder track in Oxford, a young English medical student, Roger Bannister – at twenty-five, Moss's exact contemporary – became the first man to run a mile in under four minutes. As car ownership spread, motor racing was revived as a sport whose appeal now broadened itself beyond those who had flocked to pre-war Brooklands: in a world where everything new, from jet airliners to fountain pens and kitchen appliances, reflected the fashion for streamlining, it had the excitement of modernity.

In the first years of peacetime a young racing driver could take on the mantle recently worn by the figures who had emerged from the war, dead or alive, with the aura of the knights of old: men like the legless fighter ace Douglas Bader, a byword for mad courage; Guy Gibson, leader of the Dam Busters raid; or Pat Reid, a successful escapee from Colditz

Castle, who later reflected: 'I can think of no sport that is the peer of escape, where freedom, life and loved ones are the prize of victory, and death the possible though by no means inevitable price of failure.' Moss was risking his life for his country – as some would see it – in a very different sphere of competition but exuding a similar air of courage and chivalry in the proportions that represented the British public-school ideal of sportsmanship.

He was exactly a decade into his career when a British schoolboy sat down with the solemn intention of writing his life story. On the left-hand pages of a green notebook he recorded the significant events of the driver's career to date – none of which he had actually seen, even on film: the apprenticeship, the growing international reputation, the increasingly important victories, all written out in blue-black ink with a slightly scratchy fountain pen. Opposite the words were photographs cut from the family copy of the *Daily Telegraph* and from editions of the weekly motoring magazines *The Autocar* and *Motor*, passed on by a neighbour. Stirling Moss in a Maserati, jousting with the Lancia-Ferraris in Buenos Aires; in a Vanwall, sharing victory in the British Grand Prix at Aintree with his teammate Tony Brooks; even emerging from a London church with his new bride in a cloud of confetti. And that, in 1957, was how this book began.

# CHAPTER 3

# HAMISH MOSES

Had his Scottish mother's wish prevailed, he would have been called Hamish. Instead she was persuaded to name her son after her own birthplace, a historic town on the banks of the Forth in central Scotland, midway between Edinburgh and Glasgow, where William Wallace defeated the English at the Battle of Stirling Bridge in 1297. And it was thanks to a grandfather's decision in the nineteenth century that his branch of the Moses family of Ashkenazi Jews, transplanted from Germany to London, became known as Moss.

Hamish Moses. What kind of a name for a racing driver would that have been? 'Stirling Moss' was perfect: a crisp dot-dot-dash cadence, distinctive, resonant, memorable. Easy on the tongue and with a headline-friendly surname in the bold type of tabloid newspapers: 'MOSS WINS AGAIN', 'MOSS IN A SPIN', 'JINX HITS MOSS', 'MOSS MORE THAN FRIEND, SAYS JUDY'.

The homophone of Stirling was a word with two related meanings. 'Sterling', with origins in Old English, Old

French, Medieval Latin and Middle English, was a term for the silver penny of the Norman dynasty; later it was applied to British money in general, and in particular – via 'a pound of sterlings' – to the pound itself. In the seventeenth century it was adapted to become a term of approval, meaning 'thoroughly excellent, capable of standing every test': sterling character, sterling principles, sterling qualities.

His full name was Stirling Craufurd Moss: the middle name also came from his mother, the former Aileen Craufurd, who had married his father, Alfred, in 1927. Following Stirling's birth on 17 September 1929 at 10 Westbourne Grove Terrace, in Bayswater, his parents took him to live in Thames Ditton, Surrey. His father, having given up an early venture into co-owning a garage in south London, had established a chain of dental practices around the city; its success enabled them to move to a farm called Long White Cloud outside Bray in Berkshire, with a handsome half-timbered main house, where Stirling was joined by a sister, Pat. From his fifth year onwards, Stirling was encouraged by his father to pursue a physical fitness regime that involved boxing, rope-climbing, gymnastics, swimming and rowing, under the supervision of an instructor. For both children, the advantage of living on a farm was the scope for keeping pets of all shapes and sizes, for riding ponies and horses – under the supervision of their mother, an expert horsewoman – and eventually in Stirling's case for learning to drive at the age of nine or ten away from public roads, in an old Austin 7 bought by his father for £15 and modified for use as a kind of pickup truck on the farm.

By that time he was already winning trophies in pony club gymkhanas, soon emulated by his sister. Stirling and Pat inherited their competitive instinct from both parents, who had met at Brooklands, where Alfred was a regular competitor. While studying dentistry in Indianapolis, he became the first British driver to enter the 500 Miles race, finished fourteenth in a Frontenac-Ford in 1924, and went on to compete in dirt-track racing, a world in which an Englishman was something of a novelty and a crowd-puller. But he was back in England, trying to make the garage business work, when he met Aileen in 1926; a keen showjumper, she switched to motor sport and would go on to compete in trials and rallies in Squire and Marendaz sports cars with considerable success, becoming the English ladies' trials champion.

With their parents' encouragement, Stirling and Pat began amassing an enormous collection of cups and rosettes from their showjumping victories. But Stirling's real interest, from the start, was in cars. He was five years old when his father drove him around Brooklands, and the outbuildings at Long White Cloud were full of interesting vehicles: a supercharged Alfa Romeo, a V12 Lagonda, an old Rolls-Royce, two Lancia Aprilias for daily use, one for each parent, and several machines, mostly Marendazes, driven in trials by both of them.

Stirling's early schooldays were spent at Shrewsbury House primary in Surbiton and at Clewer Manor, a prep school linked to the Imperial Service College. By the time he was ready for secondary education, at the age of thirteen, the ISC was being merged with Haileybury College, a public school set in 500 acres of Hertfordshire countryside. His predecessors at the school included the artist Rex Whistler, killed by a mortar round soon after the D-Day landings in 1944, and Clement Attlee, a future prime minister. He enjoyed games – he ran and boxed and played rugby (on the wing), although he hated cricket, which was too slow for his taste – but his academic success was limited and his years there were by no means happy ones. Various illnesses – scarlet fever, appendicitis, chronic earache and, most serious, nephritis, an inflammation of the kidneys – cost him, he later estimated, several terms' worth of education, leading to a failure to pass his matriculation exam. And he was frequently caned by his housemaster, one Major Nicholls, for minor infractions and insubordination.

It was also at Haileybury that he became aware of anti-Semitism and first heard the term 'Yid', employed as a casual insult by his schoolmates. 'Catch the Yid,' they would shout as he flew down the wing in a rugby match, which only encouraged him to run faster. In later years his British rival Mike Hawthorn would sometimes refer to him as 'Moses', the sort of joshing that was deemed acceptable in the 1950s but, whether intentional or otherwise, necessarily contained a darker undertone.

When the war came, according to the family legend, Alfred Moss invented an indoor air-raid shelter: a tent-like structure made from steel and wire mesh, intended to protect the occupants against falling masonry. Such devices became known – after Herbert Morrison, the Minister of Home Security – as Morrison shelters; more than half a million were provided free to households whose income was less than £400 a year. (The official history says that its designer was a Cambridge professor named John Baker.)

In the last year of the war, the 15-year-old Stirling was registered as a motorcycle dispatch rider. At the Royal Windsor Show, a few weeks after VE-Day, both Moss children won showjumping prizes, presented to them by King George VI;

it was just about Stirling's last competitive outing on horseback. He left school at sixteen, in the summer of 1945, and sold his possessions – including his radio, his tent and his bicycle – to his father in order to raise £140 for a Morgan three-wheeler, which he was allowed to drive using a motorcycle licence. His first four-wheeled car, acquired in 1946 after selling the Morgan, was an MG TB drophead.

Since following his father into dentistry was not an option, thanks to his failure to pass the necessary exams (even after a few months spent at a crammer), it was thought that hotel management might be a suitable career option. He worked as a junior chef at the Palmerston restaurant in the City of London, followed by spells at the Bayswater Hotel, near Hyde Park – where he called himself 'Toni' because he felt that 'Stirling' was an unsuitable name for the job – and behind the bar at the Eccleston Square Hotel in Pimlico. It was there, he told the motoring historian Doug Nye, that he learned to collect the dregs from splits of bitter lemon and tonic water in fresh bottles and resell them to unsuspecting customers for a bit of freelance profit.

But by the time he was seventeen, his mind was made up. His head was full of cars. He was going to be a racing driver.

# CHAPTER 4

# THE WHITE HELMET

In the 1940s, Grand Prix aces still wore thin linen wind-bonnets offering no protection at all against impacts; anything more substantial was deemed to be for amateurs. Hard-shell helmets would not be compulsory for racing drivers until 1952. But as soon as Stirling progressed from speed trials to hill climbs, his parents insisted that he protect himself with the sort of headgear worn by polo players, as used before the war by a number of prominent British racing drivers. His first, on loan from his father, was dark leather. But in September 1948 he appeared wearing a lid of his own: a pure white helmet with white leather earpieces and chin strap, and a small peak around which he could attach a visor to replace his aviator's goggles in bad weather.

Moss's helmet came from the hatter Herbert Johnson, of 38 New Bond Street; it was made of cork, papier-mâché and an outer shell formed from several layers of laminated resin-soaked linen, and cost five guineas. Slightly tilted as he leaned back in the cockpit, the white helmet became his visual signature in an era when racing drivers were easily identified by their individual headgear: dark brown for Fangio, pale blue for Ascari, black with a white-peaked visor for Hawthorn, tan for Peter Collins, and so on. When Herbert Johnson produced a model with a fibreglass shell in 1958, the price went up to six guineas. Later he used similar helmets from Les Leston, a former driver who had established himself as an equipment supplier.

In the final years of his career he wore pale blue two-piece Dunlop overalls; before that his kit had been mostly white, occasionally British racing green. For races in high temperatures he usually wore short-sleeved polo shirts, including a pale blue one with a waffle pattern – made by Suixtil, a manufacturer based in Buenos Aires endorsed by the great Juan Manuel Fangio and other Argentinian drivers – that he believed was more effective at dispersing the kind of extreme heat encountered in places like Sebring and Pescara; he probably acquired it in Buenos Aires after suffering heatstroke during a non-championship grand prix there at the start of that year. Like most drivers of his generation, he wore stringback gloves with leather palms. His watch, worn on his right wrist, had a distinctive bracelet formed from two thin steel bands; unlike leather, it would not absorb dirt and sweat. On his left wrist he wore a silver identity bracelet. He wore ordinary socks and shoes, usually slip-on loafers.

None of his garments offered any significant protection against fire, although by the end of the '50s the drivers were being offered a preparation that was supposed to provide some sort of flame-proofing to standard cotton overalls. The danger of fire was why he and his contemporaries disdained the idea of seat belts: they preferred to be thrown out of the car in a crash rather than risk being trapped in a blazing wreck.

Eventually he sold the white helmet in which he won the 1957 British Grand Prix to the British Oxygen Company, who had it covered in gold leaf to be preserved as a trophy. In 2009 it was auctioned for £23,000.

At Silverstone on 13 May 1950, the day of the first F1 world championship grand prix, Moss and his Cooper-JAP competed in the support race for 500cc cars, winning their heat but finishing second in the final when a piston failed on the last corner (Klementaski collection).

# CHAPTER 5

# THE 500 CLUB

He had paid his first visit to a motor-racing circuit at the age of five, when his father strapped him in for a lap around Brooklands. (That day, while peering into a car's cockpit, he leaned against the hot exhaust pipe and burned his stomach, an incident he later credited for giving him a high threshold of pain.) At the end of the war, however, it became clear that the track in the Surrey stockbroker belt was lost to racing for ever. The Byfleet banking had been breached to make a larger entry road to the factory where Hawker Hurricanes were being manufactured, while the Luftwaffe's visits had left a number of craters. The whole site was about to be sold to the Vickers aircraft company.

It was in France that proper racing first restarted after the war. In September 1945, a crowd estimated at 200,000 thronged the Bois de Boulogne on the western edge of Paris to watch a day of races contested by carefully preserved pre-war Maseratis, Delahayes, Alfa Romeos and Bugattis. Three events – their titles reflecting the agony of the preceding six years – were held that afternoon: the Coupe Robert Benoist, dedicated to the former French champion and Resistance martyr; the Coupe de la Libération; and the main race, the Coupe des Prisonniers, won by Jean-Pierre Wimille, another Resistance hero. Continental racing was back, and the following year competitions would be held on road circuits in Nice, Marseilles, Geneva, Turin, Milan, Barcelona and elsewhere. The classic endurance races were also on their way back: the Mille Miglia would return in 1947, the Targa Florio in 1948 and Le Mans in 1949.

In the UK, the resumption of activity was hindered by a law that since 1925 had prevented racing on the public roads of mainland Britain. As well as Brooklands, the other two purpose-built tracks were out of action. Donington Park in the East Midlands, also scarred by military use during the war, had been returned to its civilian owners, who showed no signs of inviting the racing world back on to their premises. At Crystal Palace, the local council had declined to permit the reopening of the circuit, claiming that the noise would upset the residents of the surrounding south London suburb.

Speed and consistency trials and hill climbs were the first competitions to reappear. The Cockfosters Rally, held on 14 July 1945, was a reunion of the tribe: various Bugattis and Alfas were disinterred, even a 1914 Grand Prix Mercedes, some of them driven by men still in uniform – a squadron leader in a Railton, a flight lieutenant in a BMW, and Major Tony Rolt MC, liberated from Colditz before he could escape in the glider he had built in the castle's loft, and now at the wheel of an ERA. A month later came the first genuine speed event, a hill climb organised by Bristol Motor Club. 'Arranged primarily for competitors, with spectators tolerated rather than encouraged, the event gave some hundreds of people their most enjoyable afternoon in a very long time,' *Motor Sport*'s correspondent wrote.

A yearning for proper racing had been expressed as early as 1941 in the letters column of the same magazine, where a reader presciently pointed out that the end of the war would leave an abundance of redundant military aerodromes, with their runways and perimeter roads offering 'ideal sites for minor sprints and road races'. Five years later those words came true when, on 15 June 1946, Britain's first post-war circuit race took place at Gransden Lodge, 10 miles west of Cambridge, on land from which Mosquito pathfinders and Lancaster bombers had only recently been taking off. Organised by Cambridge University's motor club, the meeting consisted of a dozen short races for racing and sports cars of various sizes. Victory in the event's big race went to the Bugatti of George Abecassis, who had been shot down and captured while dropping supplies to Danish resistance fighters in 1944.

There was no sign at Gransden Lodge that day of a revolution that would profoundly influence the whole of international motor racing, and which had begun with a debate about what form racing might take when the war had been won. A series of articles in *Motor Sport* proposed basing a new single-seater formula on the international Class I, for cars with engines of no more than 500cc. This would appeal to impecunious enthusiasts who could use motorcycle engines and components from small saloon cars to create their home-built 'specials'.

The idea caught on, and the entry for an early post-war hill climb at Prescott in the Cotswolds included two examples of the new 500cc racing cars: the Strang, named after its creator, a New Zealander with a garage business in Harrow, who fitted a Vincent engine behind the driver on a chassis using pre-war Fiat Topolino parts; and the Tiger Kitten, built by Clive Lones around bits from various Austins and powered by a single-cylinder JAP engine, conventionally mounted in front of the driver. 'These cars proved conclusively that 500cc cars are amply fast enough to hold the spectator's interest,' *Motor Sport* noted.

By the start of 1947 a 500 Club had been formed, a set of regulations had been drawn up and the organisers of race meetings were beginning to include events for those who saw the new formula as a cheap and interesting way to go racing. Soon the cars of Colin Strang and Clive Lones were joined by other home-built specials – the Iota, the Spink, the Fairley, the ASA, the Wharton, the Aikens and others – among which the cars built at Charles Cooper's little garage in Surbiton, south-west of London, quickly became pre-eminent.

Stirling Moss was on the way home from one of his outings in the BMW towards the end of 1947 when he persuaded his father to stop at that nondescript building just off the Ewell Road, where the dimensions of chassis frames for new racing cars were drawn in chalk on the brick walls and the concrete floor. The owner's son, 24-year-old John Cooper, and his friend Eric Brandon had designed and built a car to compete in the new low-cost formula. Like Strang, they had put the engine – their first one was a single-cylinder JAP, made in north London and mostly used after the war in speedway machines – between the driver and the rear axle, saving weight and allowing the driver to sit low in the cockpit, between suspension units scavenged from a pair of Topolinos, the two front ends welded together.

The mid-engined layout had been used occasionally before the war, most spectacularly in the Auto Union cars designed by Ferdinand Porsche. But those were big and complex cars, rugged enough to race in Grands Prix on long road circuits where the surface was often rough and uneven, and their rearward weight balance presented an unfamiliar and fiendishly difficult challenge for all but such virtuosos as Bernd Rosemeyer and Tazio Nuvolari. The first Coopers, by contrast, were lightweights, perfectly suited to the new environment in which they were being raced: the smooth, flat asphalt perimeter roads of old aerodromes.

The success of the Coopers paved the way for a generation of cars that would go on to dominate the highest levels of the sport, resetting the prevailing design philosophy – of circuits as well as cars – for generations to come. But when Stirling Moss drew his father's attention to their existence, he was simply looking at an affordable way to take the next step in racing. The new Cooper Mk II – one of a dozen being built for customers – would cost £575.

There had been an awkward exchange in the Moss household a year earlier when Alfred discovered that his son had sent off a £50 cheque as a deposit to the maker of another 500cc machine, the Marwyn, made in Bournemouth and offered as a complete car with a JAP engine for £445. That payment was stopped. But now he could see that Stirling was serious about making progress in a pursuit for which he was already showing not just keenness but aptitude. Alfred could even use his own friendship with Stan Greening, the man who made JAP engines, to get a decent unit at a favourable price. There would also be help from Don Müller, one of many German prisoners of war who had stayed behind to work on British farms. Müller had been a fitter at BMW in his native Bavaria; now, in addition to his duties as a farm-hand on Long White Cloud, he was enlisted to help prepare and run the car.

As usual, Alfred insisted that Stirling should contribute some of the cost of the car himself. But, basically, the cream-painted Cooper-JAP came as an eighteenth birthday present. When Stirling briefly tried it out on the roads of an unfinished housing estate, he discovered that the very rudimentary seat and the cutaway cockpit offered an alarming lack of support when cornering. He would need to develop a technique of steering with one hand while clutching the side of the bodywork with the other.

After an attempt to enter a hill climb at Shelsley Walsh was rebuffed on the grounds of his inexperience, he gave the little car its debut at Prescott. Packed into one of the family's horseboxes, it was towed behind Alfred's old Rolls-Royce to the Gloucestershire venue, where Stirling finished fourth in the 500cc class. A month later at Stanmer Park, a hill climb in the grounds of a stately home outside Brighton, he beat several of the same opponents, including Eric Brandon, to take his first victory in the car.

On 4 July he entered his first circuit race, at the Brough aerodrome in the East Riding of Yorkshire. There were already signs that this was becoming a serious little operation: they took the car and its methanol fuel up north on the train, and flew it back. The track was tiny – barely two-thirds of a mile – and the fee for his entry was five shillings. In heavy rain, a win in the heat was followed by first place in the final and a third win of the day in a handicap race. The day produced prize money of £15 and an approving mention in the *Daily Mail*. Further hill-climb wins at Bouley Bay and Prescott provoked Raymond Mays, a senior figure in British motor racing, to describe Moss in the *Daily Graphic* as 'the most promising of our young drivers'.

The little team at Long White Cloud had spent time working on the car, drilling components for lightness – as the Germans had done before the war – and experimenting with gear ratios, spark plugs and tyre pressures, and on 18 September they travelled to West Sussex for the day on which the old Westhampnett fighter base was to be transformed into the Goodwood racing circuit – as yet lacking grandstands, paddock shelter or a scoreboard, but already a fast and challenging track. Despite starting from near the back of a grid whose composition was decided by ballot, Stirling was in the lead by the time the field came out of the first corner and won easily, almost a minute ahead of Brandon at the end of three laps of the 2.4-mile track, so dominant that his father was able to put out a signal to slow down. Thirty guineas was his prize, along with his first interview, given to a local paper. It was the day after his nineteenth birthday, and his cake was cut on the bonnet of his car as the family celebrated.

There was a disappointment in the 500cc race at the first post-war British Grand Prix meeting at Silverstone in October, when 100,000 turned up at the Northamptonshire aerodrome. Colin Strang led from pole position in his own car but retired with a seized engine, leaving Moss to take over until an engine drive sprocket failed. But for the first time the teenager had rubbed shoulders in the paddock with the continental aces featured in the main event, including Luigi Villoresi and Alberto Ascari, who finished first and second in the latest Maseratis. A distinctive figure in the paddock was that of the portly Alfred Neubauer, the legendary manager of the pre-war Mercedes racing team, visiting England for the first time since the funeral of his English driver Dick Seaman in London a few weeks before the outbreak of war. The Germans were still excluded from motor sport, but Neubauer was thinking ahead to his team's return.

The following week's win at Dunholme Lodge in Lincolnshire, another former aerodrome, closed a season in which Stirling had won eleven of the fifteen events he entered, ending the year with only a small financial loss. He had caught the eye of many observers, including the members of the British Racing Drivers' Club, who welcomed the precocious teenager to their exclusive circle; at their annual dinner he was introduced to the Duke of Edinburgh, who showed a keen interest in his progress.

Now his father could see that this was definitely more than a young man's passing fancy, and together they agreed to take the next step. For 1949 they bought John Cooper's latest design, the Mk III, and a new Bedford van to go with it. To replace Don Müller, who had returned home to Germany, they hired a permanent mechanic, Rex Woodgate, who came to live in a caravan on the farm. The new car could be fitted with a choice of 500cc and V-twin 1000cc JAP engines, capable of being swapped between races, enabling Moss to race in two categories on the same day. Its body panels anodised in a shade of pale metallic green, the car had a seat that gave much better support for Stirling's back and thighs; nevertheless he was also now wearing a corset-like kidney support belt, 5 or 6 inches deep and with three buckles, of a kind that some top drivers, including Nuvolari, used to counteract the effect of high cornering forces.

At Goodwood in April the bigger engine provided the first win of the season in the Easter Handicap. That was an hors d'oeuvres to the support race at the 1949 British Grand Prix, now held in mid-May. In front of another huge Silverstone crowd, many of them watching from temporary grandstands, the pale green Cooper led the thirty-six entrants in the 500cc race by the end of the first lap. With an emerging young national hero at the wheel, it was never seriously challenged for the rest of the fifty-mile race. 'Another great victory for Moss,' *Motor Sport* concluded. 'Nothing, one feels, could have been more popular.'

A fortnight later, with the bigger engine installed, he travelled to the Isle of Man for the Manx Cup over the 3.8-mile circuit in Douglas, the island's capital. It was his first experience of true road racing, and in a seventy-mile contest for Grand Prix cars he put the Cooper on pole position and was soon leading by such a distance that his father was again signalling him to slow down and save the car. But with victory almost in sight, the magneto drive failed. What the day had taught him, however, was that racing on public roads offered a much more compelling challenge than dicing on a strip of tarmac around the perimeter of an old aerodrome.

# CHAPTER 6

# VOYAGE TO ITALY

In July 1949, accompanied by two friends, he set off in the Bedford transporter for his first taste of continental racing. His destination was Salò, on the shore of Lake Garda in northern Italy, where Mussolini had led his final attempt to cling on to power only six years earlier. The town was now the base of the 9th Circuito del Garda, a race on local roads running into the hills above the town, and he made his way to the organisers' headquarters to pay the £50 entry fee.

With the 1000cc engine still fitted and with special long-range fuel tanks slung alongside both sides of the bodywork, the air-cooled, chain-driven Cooper was initially the object of derision from local enthusiasts. They took one look at the funny little machine – one of only four non-Italian entries in a field of thirty-seven – and, having compared it to their own shapely Alfa Romeos and Maseratis, nicknamed it 'the jukebox'. They were examining it through different eyes after the practice sessions, in which Moss set a time that split Luigi Villoresi and Mario Tadini in the latest works Formula

2 Ferraris, each with twelve cylinders to his two, two litres to his one and getting on for twice his horsepower.

He was discovering a different world, one to which he responded immediately and instinctively. The ten-mile Garda circuit was on public roads, mostly narrow, bounded by walls, banks and ditches. If you went off, you might hit a house or a telegraph pole or tumble down a hillside. On the airfield circuits at home, young drivers could acquire bad habits that were difficult to unlearn in a less forgiving environment. Moss found the new challenge very much to his taste.

The event was organised in two heats and a final. Drawn in the first heat, run over eight laps, Moss finished third, behind Villoresi and Tadini. While the second heat was in progress – won by Count Bruno Sterzi in the third works Ferrari – Moss and his pals cut a hole in the underside of the Cooper and bent the metal out in order to direct cold air on to the magneto, which had been showing signs of overheating.

He began the ten-lap final, the only non-Italian of seventeen starters, by trailing the three Ferraris, following directly behind Sterzi, a wealthy young paper merchant from Milan who had been one of Enzo Ferrari's first customers. Noting the erratic nature of the Italian's driving, he watched from a safe distance until Sterzi finally lost control while crossing a set of tram lines, left the road and hit a pole supporting the overhead cables, snapping it in two, before the Ferrari toppled over a drop. The driver was taken to hospital with internal injuries and a broken leg. Moss battled for a while with Clemente Biondetti's two-litre Maserati and Dorino Serafini's OSCA until both retired, leaving him to take third place behind the remaining Ferraris and victory in the 1100cc class.

For Moss, the £250 prize was a big step up from the tenner

he was getting for a win at Prescott. And during his stay he was introduced to Tazio Nuvolari, the driver alongside whom Enzo Ferrari would one day rank him as the best of all time. Aged fifty-six, still competing occasionally despite the increasing symptoms of the ruined lungs that, combined with a series of strokes, would kill him four years later, the old master had watched Moss's performance with great interest.

From Italy, Stirling and his friends drove the van back across the Alps and up through France to Reims, where the Cooper was one of three entered in the Coupe des Petites Cylindrées, a race for Formula 2 cars supporting the French Grand Prix. He had negotiated generous starting money of £200; otherwise, this was a fool's errand. In a hundred-mile race over an ultra-fast road circuit, the little British cars were never going to be able to keep up with the two-litre Ferraris and Gordinis. When Moss's drive chain broke, he pushed the car more than a kilometre to the pits and a repair was made, only for the magneto to fail again. But he returned to England having breathed the rarefied air of continental competition for the first time, finding himself more than equal to the varied challenges and multiple hazards presented by racing on public roads, and definitely wanting more of it.

# CHAPTER 7

# ROYAL SILVERSTONE

It was the sight of Moss in a 500cc car that prompted the journalist Gregor Grant, the founding editor of *Autosport*, to compare him to a pre-war ace when he noted 'a touch of Rosemeyer' in the way he tackled a high-speed corner – 'the same fire and certainty that the car was always under control.' The Boy's reputation was growing fast, and at Silverstone in May 1950 he stood in a line of drivers being presented to King George VI and Queen Elizabeth in advance of an afternoon featuring the opening round of the inaugural FIA Formula 1 world championship.

Moss took part in the 500cc event, the day's supporting attraction. The programme hailed him as 'likely to become Britain's star of tomorrow', but after winning the first of two five-lap heats, cheered on by a crowd of 150,000, he had to give best in the ten-lap final to a Triumph-engined Iota driven by Wing Commander Frank Aikens, a veteran of wartime anti-submarine missions. Third came another English prodigy, the 18-year-old Peter Collins. Second place was worth £40, plus £20 for winning the heat.

The big race, carrying the honorary title of the Grand Prix d'Europe, was a clean sweep for the Alfa Romeo team, led by Nino Farina, who took the £500 first prize and the first step on his path to becoming the inaugural world champion. Their Majesties were taken round the circuit to watch the race from a variety of vantage points. When it was all over, many spectators found themselves held up for several hours while inching their way out of the car parks and through the jammed lanes around the circuit, a Silverstone experience with which several future generations would become familiar.

During the meeting Stirling also encountered Nuvolari again, and they were photographed together: a silver-haired man in a tweed jacket, shirt and tie standing next to a 19-year-old boy with a shock of dark, curly hair, wearing zipped white racing overalls with a BRDC badge proudly on his left breast. One legend on his lap of honour, the other busy being born.

His parents travelled with him on his first trip to the Monaco Grand Prix, where he greatly enhanced his reputation with wins in the heat and the final of the 500cc race, under the eyes of Formula 1's big names. They stayed on to watch the following day's Grand Prix, won by Fangio's Alfa.

In June, on the little kidney-shaped track at Brands Hatch in Kent, Stirling entered five races in the Cooper-JAP and won them all. The 500 Club's committee had helped raise the money to put an asphalt surface on a layout previously used by dirt-track motorcyclists. Each of the races was of only two laps, but five victories in a day was another milestone in Moss's career, boosting the growth of his reputation.

In the autumn the Cooper was fitted with a more powerful twin-cam Norton engine, which Moss used to beat

Raymond Sommer, the French veteran, in the 500cc race at Silverstone's International Trophy meeting. At the end of the season he was presented with the BRDC's Gold Star, awarded to the most successful British driver of the year: an extraordinary achievement for a 21-year-old, and the first of ten he would win between 1950 and 1961. Thanks to his results at Lake Garda and Monaco, he was also given the BRDC's Richard Seaman Trophy, awarded to the British driver with the best results in international competition.

The invitations to drive more powerful machinery were starting to arrive, but 500cc and 1000cc racing would remain on Moss's schedule even after he had become an established Grand Prix competitor. Prize money was coming his way, and points that counted towards the Gold Star. Over the next four seasons he would drive Norton-engined Coopers and a Kieft to three more wins in the British Grand Prix support race and two victories in the Eifelrennen over the full 14-mile Nürburgring Nordschleife. There would also be a spectacular accident at Castle Combe: while holding off Tony Rolt's two-litre Connaught in his Cooper, he braked too hard and was hit up the rear, the car throwing him out as it somersaulted, a bone in his shoulder cracking as he landed.

In 1954, his last season with the 500s, a Cooper heavily modified by the engine tuner Francis Beart carried him to six wins from eight races. A final victory at Aintree during the *Daily Telegraph* Trophy meeting would conclude his adventures in a category that had proved a useful launch pad for the careers of so many young drivers, his own most of all.

Moss in the pits at the 1951 Modena Grand Prix with his HWM teammates John Heath (centre), the company's co-founder, and Lance Macklin (Rudy Mailander/Revs Institute).

# CHAPTER 8

# TEAM LEADER

Among those impressed by his talent were John Heath and George Abecassis, two racing drivers who were also the proprietors of Hersham and Walton Motors in Surrey. Their prototype HWM had been raced by Heath in 1949, encouraging them to build a series of three cars with two-litre Alta engines for the 1950 season, to be run as a works team with a squad of drivers in which the two proprietors would be joined by the Old Etonian Lance Macklin, the Belgian jazz trumpeter Johnny Claes and the 20-year-old Stirling Moss.

The new HWMs displayed residual traces of the special-builder's magpie instincts – they were fitted with Armstrong Siddeley preselector gearboxes and front suspension parts from a Standard 12 saloon – and they were designed to be convertible for racing as sports cars; hence the driver's seat was offset to the right. But the priority was to enter an ambitious programme of continental Formula 2 races. For Moss, promised 25 per cent of his starting money and winnings, it was a first exciting opportunity to race as part of a works outfit. The team would be transported to the circuits from their base in Walton-on-Thames in a convoy consisting of an ex-army Ford truck, a Fordson furniture van and a trailer carrying their special racing fuel. Their mechanics included Rex Woodgate, who had looked after Stirling's Cooper the previous season, and a Polish ex-serviceman known as Alf Francis.

On the team's first outing, at Goodwood on Easter Monday, the cars looked handsome in their light green paintwork and yellow wire wheels but were still not fully sorted or reliable, although Moss managed to finish second in a handicap race. He was lucky to be there at all, since he had been reported by a member of the public for driving his Morris Minor on the road in an unduly flamboyant way, and was fined £15 and given a one-month ban which covered the meeting; he successfully petitioned the RAC, the sport's governing body in Britain, to allow him to keep his competition licence.

In April the team set off on its European campaign. He was running third in the Prix de Paris at Montlhéry until the engine blew up. In the Rome Grand Prix on the tight circuit around the Baths of Caracalla he was keeping up with the Ferraris of Ascari and Villoresi until a front wheel detached itself when the stub axle broke. At Reims he finished third in the Coupe des Petites Cylindrées behind Ascari and the Gordini of André Simon. Heath and Macklin were fourth and fifth, giving a boost to the team's morale.

From there they made the long journey down to Puglia, where Formula 1 and Formula 2 cars were competing together in the Bari Grand Prix. To finish third behind the Alfa 158s of Farina and Fangio, and ahead of several F1 cars, was an achievement, although Moss endured the experience of being lapped by Farina with a move of unnecessary brusqueness on the entry to a corner. As a result, the Italian ran wide on the exit, allowing Moss the satisfaction of briefly repassing him as he recovered. When Fangio, sitting behind Farina, also went by Moss, he was laughing broadly at what he'd seen.

A fortnight later they were in Naples, where Moss got the better of Franco Cortese's Ferrari and was looking a certain winner until he tried to lap Bernardo Taraschi's Giaur on the outside of a curve, only for the Italian to run wide and knock the HWM into a spin. As the car collided with a tree, Moss's face was smashed into the rearview mirror and his left knee connected with the dashboard. He managed to extricate himself quickly, fearing a fire, but his knee was broken and so were his top four front teeth. Rex Woodgate set off on foot to find him and carried him back to the pits in his arms. Two weeks later, with his leg out of plaster and wearing a set of false teeth made and installed by his father, Moss was in action once again in the Cooper at Brands Hatch.

Back in the HWM, he finished third in the Circuit de Périgueux, around the streets of the town in the Dordogne, behind two Gordinis, and the team's season concluded with a return to Lake Garda, where he was chasing the Ferraris of Ascari and Dorino Serafini when a stub axle again broke at high speed, sending a wheel into a garden by the side of the circuit. Back at the pits, Heath told Moss that since it was a wire-spoked Borrani costing £50, he had better go and get it back. The owner of the garden showed him the damage to his wall and declined to surrender the wheel until the driver had gathered enough stones to repair the hole it had made.

Moss would start 1951 as HWM's designated team leader, with Macklin in support and Heath or Abecassis taking the third of a batch of new pure single-seater cars. His win on Easter Monday at Goodwood sent the team off to Europe in a mood of optimism. A third place in Marseille was followed by fifth among the F1 cars in San Remo and third in the Monza Grand Prix, where he learned how to overcome a power disadvantage by slipstreaming Villoresi's Ferrari, earning applause from the crowd and congratulations from the Italian. At the Bremgarten circuit in Berne he finished eighth, behind the Alfas and Ferraris but ahead of half a dozen other Formula 1 cars while coping for the final hour of the race with an aeroscreen broken by a stone and then coasting across the line with a silent engine after running out of fuel 300 yards from the chequered flag.

His first continental win for the team came on the triangular 1.5-mile street circuit at Aix-les-Bains, in the second heat of the Circuit du Lac; in the final he took second place behind Rudi Fischer's Ferrari. Fourth place in Rome with a jammed throttle and a misfire, third at Zandvoort and retirements in Berlin, Rouen and Modena were balanced by wins at home in the Wakefield Trophy on the road circuit at the Curragh in County Kildare, the Madgwick Cup at Goodwood and finally a Formula 2 race at the Winfield aerodrome in the Scottish Borders. But these victories in modest home events were no longer enough.

# CHAPTER 9

# LIFE LESSONS

With ten days off between races in Bari and Naples in 1950, there were plans to take a short holiday in Capri, where he and Lance Macklin had arranged a rendezvous with the recently crowned Miss Italian Air Force. When she failed to arrive, Macklin had another idea. He told Moss that he could introduce him to Miss France. The only snag was that she was in Monte Carlo. 'He asked me to take him all the way up there to meet her,' Macklin remembered. 'That's about seven hundred miles. Unfortunately, when we got there Miss France had just left. So we went all the way back to Naples again.'

For a couple of years Macklin became his mentor in the art of living. Ten years older, a wartime naval officer and expert skier, this debonair teammate showed Moss how to widen the scope of his social life, and how, in general, to live up to the popular image of a successful racing driver. The son of the founder of the Invicta and Railton car companies, Macklin had volunteered for the Royal Navy in 1939, aged twenty, and served on gunboats. Once in the world of motor racing, his main priority was meeting girls; it was noted that he never showed too much dismay when his car broke down if it gave him the opportunity to persuade a beautiful woman to spend the rest of the afternoon in his hotel room. Sometimes he got himself into trouble. On one visit to Monaco, Moss noted in his diary the aftermath of a kerfuffle when 'the bod Macklin clouted' summoned the police.

Macklin was among those interviewed by Eamonn Andrews when Moss was the subject of *This Is Your Life* in 1959. 'I remember the first time I tried to follow Stirling round in about the same car,' he said, 'and I thought to myself, this fellow certainly doesn't hang about.' ('That's how I felt about Lance with his girlfriends, I might say,' Moss interjected.) 'We raced all over the Continent together – I think he gave me more trouble off the track than on the track. We were both pretty young men in those days and we chased around a bit together.'

At the end of their first season, they entered the 1950 *Daily Express* Rally, a thousand-mile competition around Britain, sharing the wheel of an Aston Martin DB2 borrowed from the factory, for whom Macklin had been driving in sports car races. They were not classified among the finishers, thanks to messing up the final parking and reversing tests. According to Moss, the whole thing was little more than what he described, using a favourite term, as 'a crumpet-catching tour'.

In 1955, his hopes of a Grand Prix career long over, Macklin was involved in the crash at Le Mans in which a Mercedes ran up the back of his Austin Healey and flew into the crowd, killing eighty spectators. In the late 1950s he worked as head of export sales for the Facel Vega car firm in Paris, and for a while Moss drove one of their Chrysler

V8-engined luxury sports saloons, a useful marketing boost for his friend's employers until, despite the additional patronage of Christian Dior and Ringo Starr, the company went bust in 1963.

Macklin eventually retired to Spain, but returned to England shortly before his death in 2002, aged eighty-two. As a racing driver, he was a gifted dilettante. Moss loved his company and picked up some useful tips but did not copy his entire philosophy of life. Chasing crumpet had a place, but he had no intention of allowing it to undermine the commitment to his career.

In filthy weather on the eve of his twenty-first birthday, Moss takes the chequered flag in the Tourist Trophy, beating the works Jaguars at the wheel of a borrowed XK120 (Jaguar Daimler Heritage Trust).

# CHAPTER 10

# TOURIST TROPHY

The first Jaguar XK120 off the production line went to the Hollywood actor Clark Gable, a sign of the importance of Britain's post-war export drive. Launched by Jaguar at the London Motor Show in 1948, the new sports car looked built for success on both road and track. Its name referred to the claimed top speed produced by the powerful six-cylinder engine under the bonnet of the aerodynamic roadster body, and it cost around £1,000, which was good value for a car of such performance.

Soon another of the rakish two-seaters would be playing a leading role – that of murder weapon – alongside Jean Simmons as a spoilt rich girl and Robert Mitchum as her father's chauffeur in *Angel Face*, Otto Preminger's film noir set in Beverly Hills. Before Ferrari, Maserati and Aston Martin had got their planned road cars into series production, and while Mercedes was still out of action, the Coventry firm jumped in to attract customers in the market for a car with the right blend of high performance and kerbside charisma.

Aware of the publicity value of success in competition, the company's racing department built half a dozen light-weight aluminium-bodied XK120s, three of which were prepared for the 1950 Le Mans 24 Hours. Two finished the race, in twelfth and fifteenth places. Possibly stung by the sight of two new works-entered Aston Martin DB2s in fifth and sixth, Jaguar started to take their racing more seriously. On their schedule that September was the Tourist Trophy at Dundrod, near Belfast, a 225-mile handicap race over a challenging circuit featuring narrow, uneven but fast country roads bounded by earth banks.

Having admired the XK on its racing debut at Silverstone the previous year, Moss petitioned Jaguar for a place in their works team for the TT. They turned him down, explaining that he lacked sufficient experience. Instead, after a conversation in the Steering Wheel Club, he was loaned a similar car by Tommy Wisdom, the *Daily Herald*'s motoring correspondent, a friend of his parents and an experienced amateur racer who had been watching his progress with interest. Wisdom had been offered a drive in the TT in a Jowett Jupiter, and he was curious to see how the young man would go in the Jaguar.

Moss believed he had been rejected by the factory team simply because they were afraid of the bad publicity if this increasingly popular 20-year-old should crash and hurt himself at the wheel of one of their cars. But they were clearly taking him seriously, and in the run-up to the race they lent him a car to drive on the road for a few days, allowing him to get used to its characteristics.

Settling into Wisdom's car in Dundrod, he practised in the rain on the first day and in the dry on the second, setting excellent lap times. The rain returned for race day, along with high winds. Conditions throughout the three-hour race were filthy, but by the second lap he had taken a lead over the other thirty starters and held on to it without being seriously challenged throughout the remainder of a long and demanding drive. Completing the race at an average of 75mph, he could look at the results sheet and see below him cars driven by men with far more experience: the works XKs of Peter Whitehead and Leslie Johnson, Bob Gerard's Frazer Nash, and the Astons of Reg Parnell, Abecassis and Macklin.

That evening, in a pivotal moment in his career, Bill Lyons, the boss of Jaguar, and Lofty England, the team manager, offered him a contract as their team leader for 1951. It was 16 September, the day before his twenty-first birthday.

# CHAPTER 11

# SEVEN

Like most racing drivers, Moss had his superstitions. He thought of seven as being his lucky number. The Jaguar had worn the number seven. So had his Cooper in his first win at Goodwood's inaugural meeting two years earlier. The number had now become talismanic for him. To the small boys who were starting to follow his progress, it seemed no coincidence than seven was also the number on the shirt worn by Stanley Matthews, the nation's football hero.

When Ian Fleming, who had been on the fringes of the pre-war Grand Prix circus, published *Casino Royale*, his first spy novel, in 1953, he gave his secret agent the code name 007. At the Steering Wheel Club, where racing drivers gathered and drank, Moss would be given a membership number: 0007. Later some of his memorabilia, including the mangled steering wheels from his celebrated accidents, would adorn the club's walls. He would lunch there often with friends, colleagues and rivals.

What was it about the number seven? God created the world in seven days. The Book of Revelation is full of sevens: seven seals, seven trumpets, seven angels, seven stars. The Israelites captured Jericho by marching around the walls seven times. The Talmud describes seven heavens. The newborn Buddha took seven steps. The ancient world had seven wonders. Seven cardinal virtues, seven deadly sins, seven colours of the rainbow, seven brides for seven brothers. The seventh son of the seventh son: a healer in Irish folklore (but a vampire in Romanian legend). Seven: in many cultures, a symbol of perfection.

These were the days when numbers were allocated by race organisers, but it soon became clear that his preference was something to be indulged, not least as part of his increasingly valuable box-office appeal. The number seven was on his Kieft when he won the Brands Hatch championship in 1951, on his Cooper-Norton when he won the British Grand Prix support race in 1953, on his Maseratis at the British GP itself in 1954 and 1956, on the Cooper-Climax with which he won the 1958 Aintree 200, on his F2 Porsche in the 1960 South African GP and on his Ferrari 250GT when he won the 1961 Tourist Trophy.

For all his success, his career was also noted for its many examples of bad luck: the words 'gremlin', 'jinx' and 'hoodoo' were often employed by Fleet Street journalists reporting on his latest sequence of retirements from races he had been dominating. The number seven was on the Lotus he was driving at Goodwood on Easter Monday, 1962: his last real day as a racing driver.

# CHAPTER 12

# AROUND THE CLOCK

For manufacturers with fast cars to sell in the post-war years, successful attempts on speed records made useful material for their advertising departments. Stirling's first outing with a works Jaguar was at the Montlhéry autodrome, 15 miles south-west of Paris, where the company booked the banked oval track for a record attempt. The plan was that he and Leslie Johnson would share the wheel of an XK120 in an attempt to drive for twenty-four hours at an average of 100mph, the first time such a thing had been done.

Opened in 1924, the Autodrome de Linas-Montlhéry had been the location of the French Grand Prix before the war, and its 2.5-kilometre speed bowl became a favourite site for record attempts. In 1926 the English racing driver Violette Cordery had led a team which covered 5,000 miles on the track at an average of just over 70mph in an Invicta built by her brother-in-law Noel Macklin, Lance's father.

The attempt on the around-the-clock record was Johnson's idea: he had won the 24-hour race at Spa with an Aston

Martin in 1948, and had given the XK120 its first victory at Silverstone in 1949. Born in Walthamstow two years before the start of the Great War, he was an amateur who subsidised his racing with the proceeds of a successful cabinet-making business inherited from his father. A mature man with a balanced attitude to life and sport, he had accumulated a great deal of experience in rallies and hill climbs as well as road racing. Only his business responsibilities and the lingering effects of childhood heart and kidney problems had held him back from a career as a top driver, and he provided Moss with a kind of mentoring very different from that of Macklin.

The white Jaguar roadster was the one Johnson had driven at Le Mans a few months earlier. With a crew of factory mechanics in attendance, their attempt began at a quarter past five on a Tuesday night in late October, shortly before nightfall. Both drivers took four three-hour stints, with Moss setting off first. The car's headlamps were not really adequate for night driving on a banked track at such speeds, but they maintained a good average, with Johnson setting a best single-lap speed of 126mph on the way to their final 24-hour total of 2,579 miles at an average of 107.46mph, giving Jaguar something to shout about in their newspaper and magazine advertisements.

In April 1951 Moss tackled the Mille Miglia in a works XK120, his first encounter with a race that would eventually occupy a prominent place in his personal history. Two months ahead of time, planning to examine the whole route, he had borrowed a car from the factory. But he had got no further than Ferrara – about 100 miles – when a van pulled out from behind an oncoming lorry and hit the Jaguar, damaging the steering and forcing him to limp back to England. When it came to the real thing, the experience was just as inglorious. With a Jaguar mechanic named Frank Rainbow alongside him, and having started the race at half past four in the morning in pouring rain, he had covered only 15 miles when he hit a patch of oil from the blown engine of a Fiat. He was unable to avoid hitting the stranded Italian car, the impact damaging the front bodywork. After he and Rainbow had bent the metal back into some sort of shape, they discovered that the gearbox had jammed. A local garage helped to free it, only for the bonnet to refuse to stay closed, ending their race.

Two months later he raced at Le Mans for the first time, in Jaguar's much-admired new C-type: a sports car based on the engine from the XK but with a chassis designed purely for racing. His co-driver was Jack Fairman, a 38-year-old veteran of Brooklands and the Tank Corps, who ran a precision-tool company in the Midlands and was prized as a driver less for his speed than for his virtues of steadiness, consistency and mechanical sympathy. Three cars were entered and Moss was given instructions to go out fast and try to tempt the drivers of the 4.5-litre Talbots, particularly Fangio and his compatriot José Froilán González, into overstressing their cars.

Moss was lined up in twenty-second place for the traditional start in which the drivers sprinted across the track to their cars, and had worked his way into the lead by the completion of the first lap. González repassed him, but Moss pushed so hard that the Argentinian wore out his brake linings, which had to be replaced in a lengthy stop. By midnight, after eight hours of racing, Moss and Fairman were in a comfortable lead, a lap ahead of Fangio's Talbot. Then, two-thirds of the way round the circuit, the Jaguar's engine blew up. Moss got out and walked back to the pits in the pouring rain.

It was the first of many such disappointments for him at Le Mans, but for the team the tactic of using him as the lure had worked perfectly. The beneficiaries were Peter Walker and Peter Whitehead, whose sister car claimed Jaguar's first win in the 24-hour classic, a victory with priceless publicity value.

That summer Johnson had another idea: they would use a car, and a team of four drivers, to average 100mph for a week. He, Moss, Fairman and Bert Hadley were the drivers, and this time they returned to Montlhéry with a closed XK120. Again taking three-hour spells, each of around 200 laps, they used a two-way radio to keep awake and alert. They also played tricks on each other. One night Moss covered himself with a tarpaulin, put a fuel funnel on his head, climbed onto Fairman's shoulders and wandered onto the track with the intention of scaring the passing Johnson into thinking he was hallucinating. Johnson responded during one of Moss's stints by setting up a table on the track and playing cards with Fairman, moving the table every lap in order to reduce the gap through which the Jaguar was passing at high speed. Once the pranks were done, they achieved their target: the coupé had covered 16,851 miles in seven days at an average of 100.31mph, generating more good publicity for the company.

Back in the C-type in September at Dundrod, Moss won the Tourist Trophy again, this time in more pleasant conditions. In a single afternoon at Goodwood he won the sports car race and a handicap event in the Jaguar and the Madgwick Cup in the HWM. On his visits to British circuits, where the programmes would be filled with short races, such busy afternoons were good value not just for him, in terms of starting and prize money, but for his increasing number of fans.

# CHAPTER 13

# COVER BOY

By the middle of his first year with the Jaguar works team, he was already enough of a celebrity to be featured on the cover of *Lilliput*, a magazine for men in which articles by the likes of the philosopher C. E. M. Joad and the short-story writer V. S. Pritchett and cartoons by Ronald Searle appeared alongside discreet female semi-nudes and advertisements for non-leaking fountain pens, camera film, cigarettes and pipe tobacco, underwear ('"Piloting an aircraft all day, I must have comfortable underwear," says Captain Peter Fletcher of British European Airways') and long-forgotten drinks ('Let's have a Gin and VOTRIX!'). A colour illustration of a smiling Moss, in his already familiar white helmet and with his goggles and a red-spotted yellow scarf around his neck, was on the cover of an edition in the summer of 1951. The accompanying story appeared between a review of Orson Welles's film *Macbeth* by Kenneth Tynan and a short story by Anthony Buckeridge, the author of the successful Jennings and Darbishire prep-school novels.

'With both feet pressing firmly on the floorboards we had the interesting experience, the other day, of being driven round Hampstead Heath by Mr Stirling Moss, the twenty-one-year-old British racing ace, confined on this occasion, perhaps happily enough, to the wheel of the green and white Morris Minor saloon which he uses for personal transport,' the uncredited author of the cover story wrote.

'There was a crash helmet on the back seat, but he did not put it on. He apologized, in fact, for not being able to show us real speed. The police, it seems, keep an uncomfortably close eye, quite unjustifiably, in Mr Moss's opinion, on racing motorists using the public thoroughfare. "They pinch you," he said, cautiously negotiating a bend, "if a tyre squeaks."

'There was also the matter of a summons outstanding, the result of a recent incident in Kingston, where Mr Moss and another car became involved in a collision which removed one of Mr Moss's door handles and several feet of paint. For a racing driver a summons can be a serious matter. If his licence is suspended he may also lose his competition licence, and that means no more racing, until the period of suspension is up.

'Under this cloud, therefore, we proceeded round Hampstead Heath, with one rapid burst along the North Circular Road. Mr Moss has fitted special valve springs to his Morris, giving it notable acceleration. Using the gearbox generously, and rolling his foot from brake to accelerator, he left a number of larger cars well behind, revealing at the same time a hair's breadth judgment of distance and width. "I'm fitting a supercharger soon," he told us. "Ought to get 80 or 82 out of her then."

'We were breathing a little more quickly as we returned to Mr Moss's one-room flat in a quiet, tree-lined road. At no time had we been in danger, but there was undoubtedly a certain nippiness in Mr Moss's method of getting about . . .'

Over a cup of tea, he answered the interviewer's request for an explanation of his cornering technique. '"Drifting, we call it," said Mr Moss. He sat well down in his chair. An intent look came over his extraordinarily level grey eyes. "You come into the corner, throw her over, and give her the gun. The back wheels start to slide. You've got to fight her then, or you're for it." Mr Moss, in his chair, fought her. We could hear the engine roaring, the scream of tyres.'

As the man from *Lilliput* finished his tea and rose to go, Moss mentioned that he would soon be making a film, possibly to be called *The Art of Cornering*. He invited the journalist to come along and be given a demonstration on a proper track in something a bit quicker than the Morris Minor, perhaps an XK120.

'We told Mr Moss we would bear his invitation in mind, and then drove, pretty nippily, back to the office.'

# CHAPTER 14

# THE MANAGER

In Britain's evolving post-war racing scene, Ken Gregory soon became a familiar figure at Moss's side. The elder of the pair by three years, he had left school at fourteen, joined the army in 1942 and was trained as an engineer before volunteering to become a glider pilot. In 1949 he applied for a job at the RAC, where he worked in the competitions department. He was also the assistant secretary of the 500 Club, and saw Moss race for the first time in a Cooper at Goodwood in September 1949. Soon they were sharing a table at the annual 500 Club dinner with Peter Collins, another young driver whose promise had been widely noted.

Gregory made his own race debut at Brands Hatch in 1950, driving a new 500cc car built by an engineer named Ray Martin and bankrolled by Cyril Kieft, a Welsh industrialist after whom the car was named. It showed promise, and the first sign of a business partnership between Moss and Gregory came when they took a joint interest in the company, which moved from Bridgend to a mews garage in

London's Victoria. Gregory carried on competing for two seasons, and actually won a 500cc race at Brands Hatch, but his involvement in Moss's career was gradually taking precedence.

In 1950, after the lease on Long White Cloud expired, Alfred Moss had bought another farm, in Tring, Hertfordshire, which he renamed White Cloud Farm. Moss and Gregory were spending a lot of time there, and Stirling's father endorsed the idea of Gregory becoming his son's manager, not least to provide Stirling with company on his increasing number of foreign trips; for his efforts Gregory would receive 5 per cent of the driver's earnings. Collins was taken on as Gregory's second client, which introduced no conflict of interest since the two drivers got on well.

Moss and Gregory saved on hotel bills by travelling to races towing a specially built caravan, until it became detached from Stirling's Jaguar Mk VII while they were going down a steep hill in Belgium, overturning and writing itself off. For a while they shared Stirling's flat in west London, and Gregory's girlfriends included Moss's 18-year-old sister, Pat. Taught to drive by Stirling when she was eleven, she had grown up hating motor racing, possibly because her brother was good at it. Gregory converted her to rallying, after which she gave up her successful career in international showjumping. She turned out to be as good in a rally car as Stirling was in his racers, crowned European ladies' champion five times, with outright victories in the tough Liège–Rome–Liège event in an Austin Healey 3000 and the Tulip Rally in a Mini-Cooper. She was married to the Swedish rally driver Eric Carlsson from 1963 to her death in 2008, aged seventy-three.

Gregory took his managerial duties so seriously that when Moss was racing for the HWM team at Monza on the day before a Whit Monday meeting at Goodwood in 1951, he stayed in England and drove the Kieft in practice in order to secure a place on the grid in the 500cc race. Stirling caught the overnight train from Milan to Zurich, took a morning flight to London, and was in West Sussex in time to jump into the car and win.

# CHAPTER 15

# THE SNUB

To the left, waste land in front of an abandoned factory; to the right, a container depot built on reclaimed land, stretching towards the glistening waters of the Adriatic. A line of small trees borders the road as it curves away into the distance, heading towards a lighthouse. It doesn't look much now, just a broad concrete highway leading out of the city. But it was here in Bari, under the same baking late-summer sun, that Enzo Ferrari snubbed Stirling Moss.

In the summer of 1951 Ferrari had offered the 21-year-old Englishman the chance to drive his cars in the French and British Grands Prix. It was a significant invitation, but Moss was already due to drive for HWM in Berlin on the weekend of the French race. Feeling he had to honour his commitment, he told Ferrari that he would nevertheless be available for Silverstone. Instead Ferrari offered both drives to José Froilán González, an Argentinian driver and friend of Fangio, who had arrived in Europe a year earlier. González finished second at Reims, sharing a car with

Alberto Ascari on a blisteringly hot day in the Champagne region, and claimed an historic victory at Silverstone, beating the hitherto all-conquering Alfa Romeo team for the first time in a world championship Grand Prix on a day when Moss had to be content with winning the Formula 3 support race.

Nevertheless, Ferrari invited Moss to a meeting in Modena, and would have been amused and intrigued when the young Englishman turned up in his Morris Minor, having driven the little car from London. As they conversed, mostly in very basic French, Ferrari offered Moss a drive in the team's new Formula 2 car at the Bari Grand Prix in September, possibly followed by a place in the team for the Italian Grand Prix, too – and, if things went well, a full contract for 1952. This was looking very much like his big chance.

'Stirling Moss is a very important young man,' *Autosport* announced when the news broke. 'His deeds with HWM, Kieft, Frazer Nash and Jaguar this season have not passed unnoticed by those who direct the racing programmes of Formula 1 cars. Already he has successfully tried out the BRM and at the time of writing he is probably being tested in a GP Ferrari, at the express invitation of Signor Enzo Ferrari himself. As one who has chosen to make motor racing his profession, Moss is a perfectly free agent. He cannot possibly be criticised for giving preference to any organisation which gives him excellent terms and the assurance of a regular wheel. It is known that Stirling is intensely patriotic, and would prefer to drive a British car. Nevertheless the time is now ripe for Moss to take the wheel of a Formula 1 car, and no one can possibly blame him for grasping the opportunity with both of his capable hands.'

When he and his father arrived in Bari, having flown down to Rome and taken an uncomfortable overnight train, they headed straight for the local Fiat garage where the Ferrari team had set up a base. But as Stirling tried to get into the cockpit of the brand-new two-litre car to see how it fitted, a mechanic stopped him. It had been reassigned, he was told, to the veteran Piero Taruffi, and there was no spare. No message had been sent to warn them of this change of plans. Enzo Ferrari was in Maranello, far away. Alfred Moss was furious, his son even more so.

A small measure of consolation came from David Murray, a Scottish driver, who offered Stirling the use of his own older Ferrari, but the centrally placed throttle pedal – a traditional feature of Italian racing cars – caught him out and he crashed it in practice. Fangio won the race in his Alfetta, with González second in a Formula 1 Ferrari and Taruffi third in the machine Moss had expected to drive. As he and his father set off on the long journey home, he swore never to drive for the Scuderia Ferrari. It was a vow that would last ten years.

Later in the year, during a lull in a test session at Monza, he was given the chance to try out the Alfa Romeo in which Fangio had just won his first world championship. Gianbattista Guidotti, Alfa's team manager, took him to tea in Como and offered him a place in the squad for 1952, with the present of an Alfa 1900 sports model as a lure. However irresistible it might have seemed in October, the offer would turn out to be worthless a few weeks later when Alfa suddenly announced the immediate closure of their Grand Prix team. Enzo Ferrari, too, had sent a telegram with the offer of an exclusive contract, but after what had happened in Bari he was wasting his time.

# CHAPTER 16

# SOUND AND FURY

The Monza test at the end of 1951 had been set up to allow Moss to try the BRM, the great white hope of British motor racing. The brainchild of Raymond Mays and Peter Berthon, who had built the ERAs before the war with backing from a wealthy businessman, the British Racing Motors project was being subsidised by a combination of sponsorship from British companies – about 300 of them – and public subscription. And everything about it was wrong.

An attempt to give Britain a real Grand Prix car of its own to compete with the Italians and the French, it aroused immediate enthusiasm but was riddled with misjudgements. At the end of the war Mays had been granted access to the blueprints of the Mercedes and Auto Union cars which had dominated grand prix racing from 1934 to 1939. What he didn't have were the designers and engineers who could make sensible use of them. The BRM's principal flaw was its technical complexity: a supercharged sixteen-cylinder 1.5-litre engine made a splendid noise and produced a lot of power but failed to achieve anything like drivability or even basic reliability until it was too late. And the BRM was, indeed, always late.

Mays had begun to approach backers in 1945 but the car's first run in front of the press – and other interested observers, including Moss – did not take place until December 1949, at Folkingham airfield in Lincolnshire. Six months later, the programme for the Royal Silverstone meeting announced that the day's schedule would feature a three-lap demonstration of the car with Mays himself, a successful driver before the war, at the wheel. Three months later the car was entered for the International Trophy at the same circuit, only for the driveshaft to break on the line, meaning that its competitive debut could be measured in inches. Two cars would be produced for the 1951 British Grand Prix, starting from the back of the grid after arriving on the morning of the race – late, as ever – and finishing fifth and seventh, a lacklustre result from cars that the public had been assured were world-beaters. When they were taken to Monza two months later, gearbox problems meant that neither car even made it to the grid. To the British press and their readers, the entire BRM adventure, for which so much had been promised, was now a laughing stock.

Mays had seen enough of Moss at work to be convinced that here was the brightest star of the new generation, with a strong appeal to the public, and he became intent on getting the young man's signature on a contract. Moss was wary, however, and even more so after he tried the car for himself at Folkingham. Although the engine produced an abundance of power, it was difficult to use. The brakes and gearbox were decent, but the chassis and steering were a disaster – 'unstable and alarming' in his view – and the cramped cockpit made it impossible for him to adopt his normal relaxed stance at the wheel.

There were meetings at the team's headquarters in Lincolnshire, and he agreed terms for one race in the car, the forthcoming Spanish Grand Prix in Barcelona. So he was surprised when Mays issued a press release the next day announcing that Moss would be driving for the team throughout 1952. He had told Mays that hundreds of miles of testing and development would be needed in order to satisfy himself that the car was both competitive and, more important, safe before he could think of making such a commitment.

In another reverse, the entry for Barcelona was withdrawn following the problems experienced during the Monza test. But if Moss was intent on making the jump to full Grand Prix racing while maintaining his insistence on driving British cars, the BRM looked like the only option available, and in September 1951 he accepted an invitation to try it out in a full-scale test at Monza. Broken pistons and constant overheating did nothing to improve his opinion of the car, and there was a lot of waiting around for repairs to be made and spare parts to arrive. He also listened while Mays told the public of his supreme confidence that 'next year will be a BRM year' while, in a measure of his own status, the chairman of the BRM Trust, the industrialist Alfred Owen, reassured the growing number of critics that 'there must be something to the car, otherwise Moss would not bother with it.'

At the end of the first set of Monza sessions he sent Mays and Berthon a detailed summary of the car's problems. His analysis was not entirely negative: he praised the rear suspension and the disc brakes. Hoping the faults would be rectified, and having turned down another approach from Enzo Ferrari, he declared himself ready to drive the BRM in competition for the first time in the non-championship Turin Grand Prix in April 1952. With that in mind, he had thrown himself into a further series of tests at Monza when, at the last minute, Mays and Berthon cancelled the Turin entry and ordered the personnel and the cars to return to England. They had been trying to persuade Fangio and González to join the team, and had been told that the Argentinian pair would be available to try the car at Folkingham that same weekend.

While leaving Moss frustrated, the abrupt cancellation had wider repercussions. Together with the withdrawal of Alfa Romeo, BRM's failure to show up in Turin persuaded the international sporting commission of the FIA, the governing body, that since a decent field of proper Formula 1 cars could not be guaranteed for the coming world championship, the series should be contested by Formula 2 cars, of which there were far more. The BRM was about to be rendered obsolete before it had become remotely competitive.

In June the two Argentinian stars went with the team to Albi, where both retired, and a week later Moss, still clinging to the hope that something could be salvaged, joined Fangio for the Ulster Trophy at Dundrod, to be run to the old Formula 1 rules. Once again the team arrived late, in time for no more than a couple of laps of practice, during which Moss discovered that the wandering front end made the car a terrifying prospect on a real road circuit. When he got into the cockpit the next morning, he discovered that – without telling him – Mays had switched the two machines, Fangio being given the one that had seemed to be the more likely to last the race. The trip turned into a fiasco on the starting line when Fangio stalled his engine and Moss's clutch burned out. Although both eventually managed to get going, neither finished the race. When Moss's gear knob came off in his hand during the third lap, he threw it away in disgust.

Others were getting fed up, too. 'Winston Churchill spurred on our troops during the war with his famous Victory sign,' *Motor Sport*'s correspondent wrote, 'but if Raymond Mays isn't careful he will see more vigorous signs of this sort directed at the BRM around the circuits of Europe.'

Hawthorn had led the early stages of the Ulster Trophy in his Cooper-Bristol and finished second after Taruffi recovered from a bad start to take the win in Tony Vandervell's Thin Wall Special, a barely disguised Formula 1 Ferrari. Meanwhile Mays was assuring journalists that, had the race been held four days later, the BRMs would have won easily. Once Moss was back home, he wrote to Mays to tell him that he was no longer interested.

Happy to be snapped by a newspaper photographer, Moss with Sally Weston, his girl-friend of the early 1950s, in a West End restaurant (Getty Images).

# CHAPTER 17

# CRUMPET

One evening in Monaco in the 1990s, strolling down the track between the Mirabeau and what was once the Station hairpin on the eve of the Grand Prix, the veteran Swiss journalist Jabby Crombac talked about his friendship with Stirling Moss. 'Ah yes,' he said. 'I remember particularly one year here, when we both caught the train back to Paris on the day after the race. I had my girlfriend with me. By the time we got to Paris, she was with me no longer.'

When Stirling was sixteen, his mother returned to the house unexpectedly one day and found him trying to surrender his virginity to a dental nurse named Sylvia. Ten years later, as he was nearing the peak of his fame, a newspaper columnist would write: 'Moss changes girlfriends as often as he changes gear. And he performs both feats with the ease that comes of long practice.'

In the early years of his career he was often photographed with Sally Weston, of Wimbledon, who liked it to be known that she was a member of the celebrated family of biscuit makers. Her real name was Jenifer Clair Tollit and she was the daughter of a British accountant who lived in New York, where she and her mother had visited him from their home in London each Christmas; her parents divorced in 1948.

She was nineteen and Moss was twenty-two when she told the *Daily Mail* in September 1951: 'Sometimes I'm engaged to Stirling and sometimes I'm not. Are we engaged now? You'd better ask Stirling. My mother says I don't know my own mind. Maybe it's true. I've been going about with Stirling since last April.' Moss himself added a comment: 'Just say Sally is an acquaintance.'

She was still around two years later, after he had broken his right shoulder in a crash at Castle Combe, when he sat on the pillion of his motor scooter with his arm in a sling as she took him from his west London flat to St Thomas's Hospital. The following year she was still being quite erroneously described by the *Sunday Express* as 'a relative of Garfield Weston, the millionaire biscuit-maker' and telling reporters asking about her relationship with Moss: 'We're just good friends.'

They travelled to races together, from Rome to the USA, and she was his frequent companion in London restaurants, at regular cinema visits to see films from *Johnny Guitar* to *Seagulls over Sorrento*, and at the Moss family home in Tring. Sometimes, on long drives between European races, she would take the wheel of his Jaguar saloon. She was there when he won the Mille Miglia in 1955, and at the tragic Le Mans a few weeks later, where Moss believed that Fangio had a brief dalliance with her. 'If he did, good luck to him,' he told a BBC *Great Lives* programme in which he paid tribute to his former teammate. 'He was a very charming man and he certainly had an eye for pretty girls.'

After the Dutch Grand Prix later in June they set off for a holiday in the South of France. En route they stopped off in Paris, where they broke up. She was not present at his next race, the historic triumph at Aintree. It did not end quietly and it was not, for a while, a clean break. Before the final Grand Prix of 1955 the Fleet Street papers carried stories about her apparent disappearance after flying from London to Nice on the way to a holiday in Italy. The English and Italian police were soon on the case, and Interpol was called in. An anxious Moss spoke to her mother on the phone, and the story ran for several days before she eventually turned up on the French Riviera, her presence at Mandelieu-La Napoule, where Moss had earlier spent his holiday, announced by Princess Chelita, the wife of the Siamese driver Prince Bira, with whom she was staying. After refusing to speak to reporters, Sally issued a statement expressing surprise at the furore: 'Everyone knew perfectly well where I was,' she said.

Moss was soon to be seen with Jean Clarke, a 22-year-old model and beauty-contest winner ('Miss Televisual') from Coventry, and Claudia Hall, an American actress in London looking for film parts. That August, a week after Clarke had described Moss to the *Evening News* as 'my steadiest date', he was meeting Hall. She had just flown in from New York when, after dinner at the Colony Club in Berkeley Square, his Mercedes 300SL – his company car, as it were – collided with another vehicle at the corner of Earls Court Road and Cromwell Road in Kensington.

His companion spent a night in hospital, being treated for bruising and shock. He told the newspapers that he had been taking her back to her hotel, but the location of the accident was on a direct line between the Colony Club and his flat at

8 Challoner Mansions in Barons Court. He collected her the following morning in a very different machine, his hotted-up and wire-wheeled Standard 8, whisking her to Snetterton in Norfolk, where – according to the press – they stayed in separate hotels and he came third in the Redex Trophy in his Maserati.

Curiously, Moss described himself as shy by nature. 'I wouldn't go into a room full of people if I was by myself,' he once said, blaming a lack of confidence that perhaps went back to his schooldays, and – with women – a fear of failure. If he approached a girl at a party, she might be thinking, 'I can't stand racing drivers. They're a lot of idiots.' He also placed restrictions on himself. He took his job so seriously that, for all his very public crumpet-chasing, until the end of his first marriage he made it a rule to abstain from sex for a week before a race, a challenge for a man racing on thirty or forty weekends of the year. Nevertheless, his pursuit of women, whether by more direct or indirect means, was enthusiastic and highly successful. He didn't drink, but he liked to take them to dinner at good restaurants, followed by dancing at various West End clubs. There would be visits to Les Ambassadeurs, Hélène Cordet's Saddle Room club or the Morocco.

The Steering Wheel Club was next door to the Mayfair studio of Baron Nahum, the society and fashion photographer whose circle of friends included the Duke of Edinburgh; sometimes Moss, leaving the club, would spot a model coming or going outside from a shoot with Baron and, overcoming his shyness, seize the moment. Further opportunities were offered by his keen eye at the cinema and the West End theatre; he was described as 'a bit of a Stage

Door Johnny' by one rising young actress who resisted his approaches in the '50s.

Under Lance Macklin's tutelage, his seduction technique became more refined ('Would you like to stay for breakfast?'). He had a black book containing the names and phone numbers of girls he had met around the world, and with whom he stayed on friendly terms even when they were no longer romantically attached. His dates included actresses such as Patsy Lancaster and Jean Aubrey, models such as Valerie Agnew (his frequent companion in 1956), and dancers such as Margot Hollen, a Windmill Girl, and squadrons of air hostesses whose names are lost to history. Some were sent flowers, ordered from Moyses Stevens in Berkeley Square.

He would drive them back to their flats before returning home, recording in his diary: 'Bed at 4.30am' or 'Bed at 5am'. When he took them back to his place, they found themselves in the home of a man devoted to modern design: modern furniture, modern glassware, modern blinds on the windows. After cars and girls, in whichever order, design was his obsession. (Once offered a silver trophy, he successfully asked if it could be swapped for a Charles Eames chair made of moulded plywood and leather, introduced in 1956 and the last word in contemporary furniture design.)

To the organisers of the Miss World contest, held annually in London, he was the perfect candidate for membership of their judging panel. His marking from 1956 survives in his scrapbook for that year. Among his notes on the contestants: 'Miss Great Britain: Legs bad. Speech good but affected. Miss Morocco: Cute. Miss Holland: Cute. Nice smile. Miss France: Good bottom. Miss Sweden: No bottom.'

# CHAPTER 18

# MISFIRING

The urge to race a British car was still there, despite the BRM fiasco. Now that the world championship was being contested by Formula 2 cars, there seemed to be a greater range of possibilities, although he felt that the HWMs had reached the limit of their potential. Leslie Johnson, with whom he had formed a good relationship in the Jaguar team, got in touch. In 1947 he had bought the ERA name and was building a two-litre car which would be eligible for the new series.

Johnson's G-Type ERA featured several advanced design elements and used the six-cylinder Bristol engine which was also being employed by Cooper and other F2 teams. There was a delay in its completion, but when it finally made its debut at Spa an engine blew up in practice and another, hastily flown in from England on a chartered plane and fitted during an all-night session by Johnson's five ex-RAF mechanics, suddenly expired halfway round the opening lap of the Grand Prix itself, sending Moss crashing into a kilometre post. In drizzly conditions in the wooded hills of the

Ardennes, he had started tenth on the grid and was up to fifth when the engine seized. He was lucky to emerge unhurt from the wreckage. Mike Hawthorn, in a Cooper-Bristol, came fourth, winning the Winston Churchill Cup for the best British finisher.

Further engine problems ruined the ERA's home debut in the British GP, and in a total of seven appearances the car yielded nothing better than a fifth at Boreham (where Hawthorn earned applause by leading Villoresi's 4.5-litre Ferrari for many laps until the rain stopped), a fourth at Charterhall, an aerodrome circuit in the Scottish Borders, and a fifth at Goodwood. Accepting that the car's inherent flaws meant it was never going to compete for Grand Prix honours, Moss abandoned the project.

Late in the season he tried a rival British F2 car for which the ERA had proved no match: the Connaught A-type, made at Rodney Clarke's garage in Send, near Guildford, using a modified four-cylinder Lea-Francis engine and bankrolled by the construction company heir Ken McAlpine. Three cars were entered for the Italian Grand Prix at Monza, for Moss, McAlpine and Dennis Poore, arriving via the team's trans-porter – an old bus – in the centre of Milan the night before practice was due to start. Behind a police escort, the three single-seaters had to be driven through the city and out to Monza – in darkness and, of course, without lights. The next day, Moss exploited his slipstreaming skills behind Ascari's Ferrari to set a good time in practice; he was lying a respectable seventh in the race when the engine failed. The Connaught was a decent enough car, but never likely to be outstanding.

In terms of top-line single-seater racing, the season had been a washout. Still insistent on driving a British car at a moment when Hawthorn was signing a contract with Ferrari, he decided to pin his hopes for 1953 on a new project involving a partnership between another John Cooper – not the one who had made his 500cc cars, but a former BRM designer who was now the technical editor of *The Autocar* – and Ray Martin, who had been responsible for the Formula 3 Kieft. Joined by two mechanics, Alf Francis from HWM and Tony Robinson, one of more than a hundred respondents to advertisements placed by Ken Gregory in the motoring magazines, they built a relatively simple car around chassis tubes supplied by the other Cooper, in Surbiton, and the four-cylinder Alta engine of the type used in the HWMs.

Moss was very closely involved with the creation of the Cooper-Alta Special, which made its debut at the East Monday Goodwood meeting, but it was destined to be, in his description, 'a dog', with a chassis that flexed, leading to unpredictable handling, and an underpowered engine. It looked the part but that was all, and the results in its half-dozen appearances were poor. When its clutch disintegrated during the French Grand Prix at Reims in July, firing out chunks of hot metal that narrowly missed vital parts of his anatomy while the Ferrari-mounted Hawthorn was becoming the first Briton to win a round of the world championship, he was left with no car for the British Grand Prix a fortnight later.

That was enough of that, and he invited Francis and Robinson to start again and build another car from scratch, using the same engine in a chassis acquired from Cooper's in Surbiton. They finished the second Cooper-Alta within twelve days, in time to set off for the Nürburgring. Sixth place in the German Grand Prix, far ahead of the other British entries, was respectable but nowhere near to matching the Italians. Looking for more speed, Francis converted the engine to fuel injection and a nitro-methane blend, but at Sables d'Olonne, on a 1.5-mile circuit laid out around a park and a small lake halfway down France's Atlantic coast, Moss could do no better than an unimpressive third against a weak field.

Next was Charterhall, where his presence was welcomed by the *Newcastle Journal*, whose reporter attended the practice session: 'Among the early birds was Sterling [*sic*] Moss, who drove up to the airfield in a sleek Jaguar, which he manoeuvred and parked in a manner reminiscent of track driving. He wore an open-neck vest, trousers clipped at the ankles and boxer-style boots, and in between inspecting his Cooper munched a peach and carried petrol tins around. When the time came for his trial he pulled on green overalls, goggles and crash helmet.' Alas, the engine of the Cooper-Alta Mk II engine gave trouble throughout the day.

At the Italian Grand Prix, the improved top speed allowed Moss to dice with Felice Bonetto's Maserati on the long straights at Monza, but half a dozen pit stops – to fix a leaking fuel tank, among other problems – pushed him down to thirteenth place. After a few more desultory races and hill climbs on home soil, the car was put away for good. It had been no improvement on its equally misbegotten predecessors in two largely wasted seasons.

In those two years he had entered an astonishing ninety-six events, but all the Formula 3 wins at home and abroad – and a third consecutive BRDC Gold Star, presented to him by the Duke of Edinburgh at the club's annual dinner – could not disguise the fact that his progress had stalled, while that of his closest British rival had surged ahead. Some were asking if his early success had been a flash in the pan, if he was too hard on his cars, or if his driving was too wild. There had been disappointments everywhere, even the major sports car events – the Mille Miglia, Le Mans and Goodwood's Nine Hours race – providing one episode of thwarted promise after another.

The first book devoted to his career had just been published – *Stirling Moss*, written by Robert Raymond, with his co-operation – and a review in *Autosport* had concluded encouragingly: 'One wonders how many similar works will follow, to chronicle the story of achievements yet to come.' Still, it was Hawthorn who now had a seat in the championship-winning team, who had actually won a Grand Prix, and whose £4,000 Ferrari road car – on loan from the factory, as exotic in looks and performance as in price – was the subject of admiring articles in the motoring magazines.

It was the rival whose smiling face was now appearing in advertisements: 'Wherever followers of motor racing gather, talk turns sooner or later to Michael Hawthorn, Britain's brilliant new racing star. Michael Hawthorn uses and recommends ESSOLUBE motor oil.' In the Moss camp, that would have hurt.

# CHAPTER 19

# NATIONAL SERVICE

Exempt from compulsory national service in the Britain of the 1950s were those whose work was deemed essential to the post-war effort to rebuild the nation: farm labourers, coal miners and merchant seamen. And, it seemed, young racing drivers.

A system of peacetime conscription into the armed forces took effect from January 1949, requiring all healthy males between the ages of seventeen and twenty-one to spend eight-een months in the armed forces and then remain on the reserve list for a further four years. A year later, in response to the start of the Korean War, the period of service was extended to two years and the time spent in reserve reduced to six months. Also spared the call-up were those who could produce med-ical evidence showing them to be unsuitable material. Special deferrals were sometimes granted.

As well as the Korean War, the call-up would involve late-imperial conflicts like the Mau-Mau uprising in Kenya or action against Malaya's National Liberation Army and the EOKA insurgents in Cyprus. Without those unwanted excitements, national service was generally thought to be tedious and unproductive, but the burden was supposed to fall evenly on all sectors of society.

Sometimes the newspapers would spot what might have been a case of dodging the obligation via some form of privilege. Politicians were alerted, and the story would be whipped up into a scandal. Racing drivers, living a glamorous life that involved travel to exotic places and perhaps driving for the glory of foreign teams, were obvious targets for such paroxysms of populist indignation.

Tony Brooks, born in 1932, was not yet a headline name, so his medical exemption on the grounds of his varicose veins passed unnoticed. Greater attention was paid to Peter Collins, who sidestepped the call-up in 1953 by going to live in Paris, acquiring a resident's permit and using his contacts to secure a job with the French distributor of Aston Martin, for whom he had been driving in sports car races. A leader writer in the *Daily Mirror* and a columnist in the *Sunday Chronicle* fulminated against his apparent refusal to do his patriotic duty, but those were pinpricks compared with the subsequent assault on his close friend Mike Hawthorn, who had also been trying to keep out of the country.

In February 1954, while Hawthorn was away racing for Ferrari in Argentina, a question in Parliament from William Robson-Brown, the Conservative MP for Esher, set off a barrage of accusations from both flanks of the national press, led by the right-wing *Daily Express* and the left-wing *Daily Mirror*, whose editorial was headlined: 'Catch this dodger!' Invited to comment, Hawthorn's father explained that after passing a medical examination in 1952, his son had requested a short deferral to allow him to take an engineering course, and had then been informed that his call-up had been cancelled altogether. But questions continued to be asked about whether the 25-year-old was spending so much time racing abroad in order to avoid his military obligations. The row went on for the rest of a year in which Hawthorn returned to England during the summer for the funeral that followed his father's death in a car crash and then again for a kidney operation at the end of the season. A subsequent medical gave him a grade four rating, which let him off the hook.

Before the Hawthorn business was over, however, Moss was dragged into it. He would have been eligible first for the peacetime prolongation of wartime conscription, which continued until 1948 and applied to males of eighteen and over, and then for its successor, national service. Had he applied for a deferral, he could notionally still have been eligible until the end of the scheme on 31 December 1960. But the childhood bout of nephritis, which had cost him part of his schooling, allowed him to claim a medical exemption.

In 1955, when he was driving for Mercedes, the story blew up in the papers and in Parliament. Manny Shinwell, the left-wing Labour MP and former Minister of Defence, had raised the matter in the House of Commons, proclaiming: 'When I hear of these daring and courageous young people going abroad, racing around tracks to the danger of their lives, and when I hear of their physical incapacity, I wonder. I should have thought that if they are capable of doing one thing, they are certainly capable of doing the other.'

In response, Alfred Moss sent Shinwell and every other MP his son's medical records in order to demolish the suspicion that Stirling had been unpatriotic. In a statement to the press, he said: 'Owing to the linking of Stirling Moss's name with certain allegations made in the House of Commons I feel that, as he is in America and unable to defend himself, I, as his father, should put the defence of his case. On August 16, 1947, at High Wycombe, Stirling was medically examined under his national service call and was, unfortunately, graded three, owing to kidney trouble. A few months previous to this date he volunteered for the R.A.F. and was turned down for the same reason.'

In the end, the row subsided. Public opinion appeared to have been swayed by the belief that Moss, Hawthorn and Collins brought more prestige to Britain by excelling in a highly competitive international sport than by wearing khaki and learning how to salute an officer or strip down a Bren gun.

# CHAPTER 20

# SALESMAN

The letter was put up for sale at a London auction of automobilia in the 1980s. Dated 24 March 1954, it was a file copy of a contract renewal between Shell-Mex & BP Ltd and the 24-year-old Stirling Moss, signed by the driver in an early version of what would become a swiftly executed but always legible signature. Since before the war, oil companies and tyre manufacturers and makers of brake linings and spark plugs and other components had sought to use racing and its heroes in their publicity material, often adding significantly to the drivers' earnings.

BP's sponsorship of Moss would last many years, sometimes requiring him to spend a day cutting the ribbons at the openings of new service stations, hopping from one to another in a helicopter. And as the advertising industry prospered in the post-war years, companies sought celebrities willing, for a substantial fee, to be linked to their products. Denis Compton advertised Brylcreem. Reg Harris promoted Raleigh bikes. Stanley Matthews assured his fans that he smoked only Craven "A" cigarettes.

By the end of 1950, when he was twenty-one, Moss's earnings were already topping £5,000, the equivalent of about £170,000 today. This included starting money, prize money, bonuses and the proceeds of his commercial endorsements. His early sponsorships included Lucozade, the popular energy drink, Nenette, a car-polishing brush, and, like Matthews, Craven "A" – he was a light smoker throughout most of his career, perhaps four or five a day, including one when he got out of the cockpit after a race, and the tobacco company paid him £500 for his endorsement. Two years after the launch of commercial television in the UK, he appeared, along with the comedian Tommy Trinder and the cricketer Alec Bedser, in the first series of TV advertisements for Coca-Cola; as a virtual teetotaler during his career, he was certainly a regular consumer, once estimating that he drank around 150 gallons of the stuff a year, or about four pints a day.

At the end of 1952, in a promotional stunt organised by the Rootes Group, he drove a cumbersome Humber Super Snipe through fifteen European countries, starting in Norway and ending four days and 3,800 miles later in Portugal, accompanied by a mechanic and his regular Alpine Rally navigator, John Cutts. Seven years later he travelled to Paris to participate in the launch of a new midget racing car called the Micromill at the Palais des Sports, for which he received 380,000 francs (this was the last year of France's *anciens francs*), then worth about £500, to race against a handful of his regular rivals on an indoor track.

There were commercial ventures of his own, too. Beefburgers were a novelty in Britain when Moss opened a restaurant in March 1957 under his father's central London dental surgery on William IV Street, close to Trafalgar

Square and just behind the historic church of St Martin-in-the-Fields. Journalists flocked to watch the Moss family cooking for the photographers and reported on the modern design and decor, with customers able to obtain a cup of coffee from a press-button machine. The following year he and his father tried a scheme to breed chinchillas on the Tring farm: paparazzi at London Airport snapped Stirling and his new wife returning from a winter sports holiday in matching chinchilla coats.

He was always up for a novel project. In 1961 he performed the ceremonial opening of what the *Daily Telegraph* described as 'a high-speed car laundry' – a pioneering car wash and valeting facility. 'With this new automatic system, a car can be completely cleaned, inside and outside, in three to five minutes, at a cost of from nine shillings to 12s 6d. Mr Hilton Lowndes, 37, from New Zealand, who has financed the £25,000 "Auto-Magic" washing installation in Brompton Road, hopes that in a few years the driver who washes his own car will be as rare in Britain as he is in the United States.'

Those who paid for Moss's presence were always given full value, although he stayed not a minute longer than the contract stipulated. If the fee was right, he would go anywhere and do most things, particularly if they involved judging beauty contests or meeting starlets.

Moss and Alf Francis (left), formerly Alfons Frantisek Kowalewski, conferring in the pits during practice for the 1954 German Grand Prix (Getty Images).

# CHAPTER 21

# THE MECHANIC

Alf Francis took his work seriously. During a pit stop at one grand prix, he punched a young mechanic for getting in the way as he tried to fill Moss's car with fuel. He knew what he wanted, and he had a short fuse. In Moss's search for a car that would give him a chance of winning grands prix, the crew-cut Francis became a trusted helper.

Born Alphons Frantisek Kowalewski in a village outside Danzig (later renamed Gdansk) in 1918, the son of a garage owner, he arrived in Britain during the Second World War, enlisting in the 1st Polish Armoured Division. When peace came, he anglicised his name and joined the HWM team as a mechanic. Impressed by his enthusiasm and ingenuity, as well as by his strong opinions, Moss had hired him for the abortive Cooper-Alta project; he and Tony Robinson also looked after Stirling's Formula 3 cars.

'I got on well with him,' Moss said, 'but he was a difficult man in every way.' Nevertheless, they struck up a good working relationship and in 1954 Francis took charge of Moss's private Maserati, working closely with the factory engineers and mechanics. When Stirling signed with Mercedes a year later, he hoped that Francis would go with him. This would have been difficult to negotiate, if not impossible, but in any case Francis's detestation of Germany and Germans, against whom he had been fighting ten years earlier, removed all need for discussion.

When it came to cars, Moss respected his experience and his views, even when he disagreed with them. A shrewd remark from the mechanic in 1954 influenced him to alter his driving style by adopting a lighter touch on the brakes. Francis had been watching the way Fangio drove and passed on his observations.

He was demanding and sometimes short-tempered but he worked enormously hard and shouldered the burden of driving a transporter the length and breadth of Europe, in the days before motorways. This was the classic ethos of the racing mechanic: an indifference to hours worked or energy expended in the face of the only imperative, which was to get the car to the line in good shape, whatever inconveniences that might entail.

Sometimes, however, even Francis could find the demands unreasonable. In the summer of 1956 he towed Moss's Maserati on a trailer behind a Standard Vanguard from London to Modena, dropping it off at the factory for a rebuild before returning in a journey that included a run of 500 miles from Chambéry to Calais in twelve hours. Once home he went straight to work on stripping down his employer's little Cooper 'Bobtail' sports car, which had been suffering from seemingly intractable handling problems. He was in the middle of the job when Ken Gregory phoned, ordering him to have the car at Reims the next day, ready for Moss to take out in practice for the twelve-hour race. Having tried to explain that he had not been warned of this possibility and that there was no time to set the car up properly, he swallowed his frustration and did as requested, enlisting the emergency help of John Cooper, the car's manufacturer and a kindred spirit: 'One of those people who look at you blankly if you talk about a 48-hour week or every other Saturday off,' as Francis put it.

Once he and the car had arrived at Reims, there were endless demands to change this and that. Then came an order to take the car on to Rouen for the following weekend's race. Again there were problems, and this time Francis's exasperation boiled over. He offered his resignation, which was immediately accepted. Moss wrote a cheque for £100 on the spot and told him: 'If you ever need any help or assistance, don't forget I am still your friend.'

They were reunited before the end of the decade, with Francis tending to the race-winning Coopers and Lotuses that Moss drove for Rob Walker's team. Together they enjoyed finding ways to make these privately owned machines go faster than the cars of the works teams. By virtue of their association, Francis became so well known that his account of his life in racing was published in 1959, with Moss providing the foreword.

After leaving the Walker team he moved to Italy, collaborating with the gearbox-builder Valerio Colotti and attempting without success to resurrect the moribund ATS F1 team, which had emerged in 1962 after a schism within the Ferrari hierarchy. His last years were spent in the United States, where he built and restored racing cars. He died in Oklahoma City in 1983, aged sixty-five.

# CHAPTER 22

# SEBRING

Rob Walker, the whisky heir who would later become Moss's patron, attended the 1954 Sebring 12-hour race with the Aston Martin team. It was almost as much a social event as a sporting contest, and Walker was delighted to note, in an account of the trip written for *Motor Sport*, the arrival of Gerald Lascelles, a first cousin of the Queen of England and a future president of the British Racing Drivers' Club, and his wife Angela. They had flown in from their sugar plantation in Barbados and agreed to keep the British team's lap chart.

Walker, who had raced at Le Mans before the war and tended to do things in style, travelled from Palm Beach to Sebring in transportation arranged by the wealthy sportsman Briggs Cunningham: 'We were a party of seven, so nothing very much in the way of cars was required. We only had two Continental Bentleys, a Vignale-bodied Cunningham, and one of the very latest Ghia V8 coupés . . .'

Sebring had begun hosting its sports-car race, which started in daylight and finished at night, in 1950. Just as

Britain's post-war racing drivers had exploited the availability of disused airfields, so the Sebring circuit was laid out on the wide concrete runways of a former US military air base in central Florida. Four years later, on his first trip to race on the other side of the Atlantic, Moss had become the first non-US driver to win the race, after being invited by Briggs Cunningham to take the wheel of a little 1.5-litre OSCA, imported from Italy. His co-driver was Bill Lloyd, a cousin of Cunningham's wife, who had raced MGs and Porsches for several years in the US and had finished fifth at Sebring a year earlier, sharing the same OSCA with Cunningham himself.

Moss and Lloyd wore out the car's brakes early in the race, requiring the drivers to throw the car sideways into every sharp corner in order to slow it down. Despite that handicap they managed to outlast the more powerful but less reliable cars of the works Lancia and Aston Martin teams, the victory extending Moss's fame into a significant new market – one in which he would feel very much at home. He had driven the last four-hour stint, after nightfall, not only with no brakes but no clutch either.

Rob Walker concluded that the Moss/Lloyd victory had been generally popular. 'It ought to have been, anyway, as it should have satisfied and consoled all participants. It was an American entrant, with a British and an American driver in an Italian car. What more could you want? I know – an all-British win.'

# CHAPTER 23

# THE GREEN MASERATI

'I will never go foreign so long as there is anything on wheels produced in England,' he had told the press towards the end of 1953. But now, while he was aboard the *Queen Mary*, returning home from a Jaguar-sponsored trip to Mexico and California, followed by a brief holiday in the Bahamas, a cable from his father announced the purchase of a new Maserati 250F with which he could take part in the 1954 Grand Prix season.

According to Ken Gregory, Moss's morale had been 'at rock bottom'. They had applied without success to Mercedes-Benz for a seat in their new Formula 1 team, and had tried all the available British cars at a special test session, concluding that none would be competitive. Another invitation from Enzo Ferrari, who had lost Ascari – the reigning world champion – to Lancia's new team, was declined. They had asked for a place in the Maserati team, but were rebuffed: Omer Orsi, the team's owner, already had a full complement of three drivers, all from Argentina – Fangio, Onofre Marimón and Carlos Menditéguy – and indirectly subsidised by the Perón

90

government, with which he had business arrangements. Instead Orsi was willing to sell them one of the two machines being built for private owners. Moss's manager and his father agreed the price of £5,500, for which Stirling himself would be liable.

Alf Francis made the journey to the Maserati headquarters in Modena, where he spent six weeks watching the factory personnel build up the car. After some argument, the company's chief mechanic, Guerino Bertocchi, agreed to get his men to move the throttle pedal from its traditional Italian position in the middle, between the brake and the clutch, to the right. Further grumbling preceded an agreement to move the seat back to allow for a straight-armed driving position. Moss also flew in to observe the final work. The bodywork was painted, as he had specified, in a pale version of British racing green – albeit a sicklier shade than he had specified – with red and white rings around the nose. A lucky horseshoe and small Union Jack stickers would be added to the flanks. Francis set off back to London with his precious cargo loaded into the team's Commer transporter.

Import duty, which would have significantly increased the car's cost, was avoided by the application for a temporary permit issued on the understanding that its owner would be spending a minimum of half the year out of the UK. Given Moss's commitment to an increasingly international schedule, both with his own team and with Jaguar, that seemed straightforward enough, as did the stipulation that any future sale could not be to a British buyer.

Moss liked the car straight away, but its debut in Bordeaux taught them one swift lesson. In wet conditions, Dunlop's tyres were not good enough. A switch to a set of Pirellis, bought on the spot from the Italian company's representatives and fitted halfway through the race, gave an immediate improvement, allowing Moss to make two laps back on the leaders and finish fourth. Before the next race, Silverstone's International Trophy, there was another on-the-fly switch, this time from Italian brake linings to Ferodo, although rear suspension failure led to his retirement. At the Aintree 200, Moss tested Francis's patience by insisting on a higher gear ratio; the switch took twelve hours to accomplish and turned out to make the car slower, requiring a change back to the original. After finishing the work at six o'clock on the morning of the race, Francis handed the car over to Moss, who walked away from the field to record his first victory in a 250F, and his first in an F1 car of any kind.

In recognition of the mechanics' efforts, Moss and Gregory gave them train tickets to London and had the transporter driven down to meet them. There they would take over for the road journey to the next race, in Italy the following weekend. That was the Rome Grand Prix on the Castel Fusano circuit, where the final drive failed when Moss was in second place. At Spa for the Belgian GP – where Francis decked a Maserati mechanic for trying to help during a pit stop – he finished third and scored the first world championship points of his career, after Bertocchi had lent them a spare set of Pirellis, again replacing the Dunlops. But he was disconcerted to find out that Fangio, the winner, had been allowed to run the engine of his works 250F up to 8,000rpm, whereas his own strict limit, prescribed by the factory for private owners, was 7,200.

Returning to Silverstone for the British GP, he was told by Omer Orsi that he could now run the engine up to 7,800;

if it blew up, the factory would rebuild it and bear the cost. Making good use of the extra revs, he had overtaken Fangio, now in the cockpit of a Mercedes, and was about to challenge González's Ferrari for the lead when the transmission broke with ten laps to go. A week later, in the non-championship race at Caen, he finished a disappointing second, losing the lead to Maurice Trintignant's Ferrari after the Maserati's handling deteriorated in the closing stages.

The problems could not disguise the quality of his performances and Orsi, now looking for a replacement for Fangio and impressed by what he had seen, offered him a deal: they would enter his car under their banner, allowing Francis to enlist the support of the works mechanics and giving access to the latest modifications. The arrangement began with the German Grand Prix, where the 250F appeared in the factory's red livery, distinguished by green and white bands around the nose, although the engine ran its bearings on the second lap, when he was lying third. For the team, the weekend was marred by the death of Marimón, Fangio's protégé, after his car went through a hedge and plunged down a steep bank.

While Moss's engine was being rebuilt and the car generally refettled in Modena, Orsi lent him a works car for the non-championship Gold Cup at Oulton Park. It arrived too late for the practice sessions, forcing him to start from the back of the twenty-car grid, but by the fourth of the thirty-six laps of the Cheshire circuit he was in a lead that he held comfortably to the finish. 'Moss's luck changes,' *Motor Sport* reported, adding that his success had earned 'a splendid ovation from the northern crowds'.

A week later his own car was ready for another non-championship race, the Circuito di Pescara on the 16-mile track used before the war for the Coppa Acerbo races. His diary recorded the trip in detail. En route, he visited Modena to negotiate with Orsi and to try out Maserati's new two-litre sports car at the Imola circuit. Late that afternoon he drove the car down the Adriatic coast to Pescara, arriving in time for dinner with Pete Ayles, a flying instructor who had arrived in a single-engined Cessna with which Moss was trying to accumulate enough air miles to get his pilot's licence.

The next morning he set out to learn the long, very fast circuit, completing five laps in the 250F. There were only thirteen entries for the race, including works Maseratis for himself and Luigi Musso. On Saturday he rose at a quarter past seven for breakfast and headed to the circuit for the second practice session. He noted all the settings – axle ratio, carburettors, plugs – and the fact that the engine was letting water into one cylinder. Nevertheless, he set the fastest time, more than twenty seconds quicker than the nearest challenger, and a new engine was to be brought down from Modena and fitted before the race.

On Sunday he was again up early for a race that began at five past nine. After a poor start, he recovered quickly to take a lead that looked certain to give him victory before a small oil pipe broke and stranded him out on the circuit. His teammate Musso won, ahead of the Gordini of Jean Behra and Harry Schell's private Maserati, while Moss went for a swim. 'Called in at the race dance, dead loss. Bed at 12.30,' he recorded in his diary.

Early on Monday morning he and Pete Ayles took off in the Cessna for Rome, where they refuelled before heading for another stop in Florence. In the late afternoon they arrived in Cannes, where Moss was staying at the Gray d'Albion, a nineteenth-century hotel which had enjoyed its heyday in the 1920s and 1930s. Used as a hostel for refugees after the Second World War, it had not quite recaptured its former glory. Dinner with Prince Bira and his wife was followed by a trip to the cinema to see *The Conqueror*, a vastly expensive flop starring a spectacularly miscast John Wayne as Genghis Khan. The next day he was up early: 'On the beach at 10, water-skied twice, lunch and left at about 3.10 and to Geneva at about 5.30.'

As heavy rain fell on the tricky Bremgarten circuit, where trees lined the roads and some stretches were cobbled, he set the fastest time in the opening practice session for the Swiss GP, ahead of Fangio's Mercedes and González's Ferrari. In the dry the following day he was still fast enough to book a front-row starting position and he was in second place behind Fangio when his oil pump failed. But this, he felt, was the weekend on which his performance had really impressed Alfred Neubauer, who was supervising Mercedes' successful return to the sport.

At Monza, in front of the Italian crowd, he qualified once again for the front row, this time alongside Fangio and Ascari, who had made a temporary return to Ferrari while awaiting the completion of the new Lancias. A spectacular dice in the opening stages between these three and Villoresi's Maserati appeared to have been settled in Moss's favour, and he was leading Fangio by twenty seconds with only a handful of laps to go when a pipe from the oil tank broke, robbing him of his first victory in the world championship. Coasting to a halt just short of the line, he pushed the car home to finish tenth. In his disappointment, there was the consoling thought that now he was a Grand Prix winner in all but name.

While leading from first lap to last in the 1954 Goodwood Trophy, Moss and the Maserati 250F demonstrate their complete command of the four-wheeled drift (George Phillips/Revs Collection).

# CHAPTER 24

# THE DRIFT

Earlier generations of grand prix stars – the Nuvolaris and Caracciolas – had driven while hunched forward in the cockpit of their heavy cars, needing to exert all the power of shoulders and forearms to turn their large steering wheels without any form of power assistance. Dr Giuseppe Farina, the first world champion, was different. His personal interpretation of racing etiquette may have left much to be desired – and was certainly not something for younger drivers to copy, as Moss had discovered on his first visit to Bari in 1951 – but his style at the wheel was a different matter. The young Englishman had been watching the way the Italian veteran sat back, with his arms straight out in front, looking completely unruffled. Not only a more elegant posture, it was also more effective.

As racing cars became lighter and the track surfaces smoother, a more delicate touch began to pay dividends. 'The veteran who designed the New Look of modern race-driving technique' was how Moss described him in his *Book of Motor Sport* in 1955. 'Now everybody does it. At an early point in my own career I made no bones about copying Farina's smooth, relaxed style.' He became the Italian's most successful disciple, particularly after he had got his hands on the Maserati. The open cockpits of the 1950s allowed spectators a clear view of the drivers at work, so Moss could be seen to be achieving his fast lap times in an unusually serene style for a racing driver. This, as much as the white helmet, helped create his image and contributed to the response he evoked from the public.

He was the right size, which helped. Hawthorn, more than half a foot taller, crouched at the wheel like a pre-war ace. 'I adopted a rather hunched driving position quite early in my career as most of the cars I drove were too small for me and I had to keep out of the wind,' he wrote. 'Gradually it became a habit.'

It was with the 250F that Moss perfected his mastery of the four-wheel drift, the art of setting a car up for a fast curve and pushing the tyres a fraction beyond the limit of their adhesion, using the throttle to guide the car through the bend with the front wheels pointing along the longitudinal line of the car, making corrections with just a touch of opposite lock. This refined approach was very different from the cruder sliding technique favoured by drivers who would leave a corner with their cars at an exaggerated angle as brute power overcame minimal grip, inducing a level of friction that wasted momentum and rubber. Drifting required great sensitivity to the car's behaviour, and it was much easier to execute with a straight-arm posture in the cockpit and fingertips rather than fists on the wheel. It also needed something like the 250F: a responsive car with no handling vices.

Who invented the drift? Some said Tazio Nuvolari, whose front wheels seldom seemed to be pointing in the actual direction of travel. Fangio was certainly its master. Moss watched him closely, studied the subtleties of his approach, and became his equal.

Eventually, as the design of racing cars changed, the technique would become obsolete, or at least applicable only to the cars used in historic racing. While it lasted, it gave spectators a clear view of something both aesthetically satisfying and clearly beyond the ability of the ordinary mortal. The four-wheel drift belonged to an age when elegance and virtuosity went hand in hand. With Moss, it was as much of a characteristic as the way he walked or talked.

# CHAPTER 25

# VERSATILE

He was never a motor-racing snob. In 1951, already recognised as Britain's most promising driver and being courted by Enzo Ferrari, he shared a friend's Morris Minor convertible in the Chiltern Night Rally, missing out on a prize through a map-reading error but, as he put it, 'enjoying ourselves regardless'. His versatility was one of his greatest assets. He had grown up with parents who entered trials and rallies, not the most glamorous forms of the sport. Curiosity about design was a quality he had in abundance, and the range of machinery in which he competed throughout his career was astonishing. He could step into almost anything and make it go faster.

His first rally had been a light-hearted 'crumpet-catching tour' with Lance Macklin, during which they had made themselves unpopular with other competitors by the boisterous tactics they employed to make up time after oversleeping. In 1952 a more serious proposition came from the management of the Rootes Group competitions department, inviting him to take part in the eight-day Monte Carlo Rally in one of their Sunbeam-Talbot 90 sports coupés.

He took along *The Autocar*'s John Cooper and the secretary of the BRDC, Desmond Scannell, to share the driving. Blizzards and sheet ice were among the hazards encountered that year, and in the Alps they had to make up time after getting stuck in a snowbank with Moss at the wheel, freed only with the help of a farmer and a pair of oxen, but they were delighted to finish second overall. Moss's fee from Rootes was an unimpressive £50, but it had enlivened the off-season, as did his first experience of a cross-country trial a few weeks later, coaxing a Harford Special up a muddy hill in Derbyshire with Cooper again alongside him as ballast.

He had enjoyed the rallying enough to enter his own Jaguar XK120 in the three-day Lyons–Charbonnières event, co-driving the green and cream car with the journalist Gregor Grant, and finishing second in their class. He was in a Sunbeam-Talbot for the six-day Alpine Rally in July, this time with John Cutts as his co-driver. They finished sixth as part of a Rootes squad, now also including Mike Hawthorn, which won the team prize. In November he was back in the XK120 for the RAC Rally, finishing thirteenth with Cooper as his navigator.

By 1953 his diary was filling up with commitments to the international racing calendar, but he found room for the Monte Carlo and Alpine rallies. The weather was milder that year: he, Cooper and Scannell finished sixth in the Monte, while he and Cutts again finished the Alpine event – in a soft-top model named the Sunbeam-Talbot Alpine in recognition of the previous year's success – without incurring penalty points, for which they were awarded their second Coupe des Alpes.

While Alf Francis was preparing his Maserati 250F for the 1954 grand prix season, Moss was reunited with Cooper and Scannell for the Monte, in which they finished fifteenth. That year's Alpine Rally, however, provided one of the most dramatic episodes of his career. He and Cutts won their third Coupe des Alpes in a row, earning them a special gold trophy, but to get it Moss had to drive a flat-out stage across a series of mountain passes including the Iseran, the Croix de Fer, the Glandon and the Galibier – all more celebrated as climbs on cycling's Tour de France – in filthy conditions with only second and third gears remaining in the car's four-speed box. And then, through surreptitious manipulation of the over-drive button, Moss had to demonstrate during a brief drive with an official that the car still had all its gears, thus satisfying the requirement to finish the event in the condition in which it had started. It was, he said, the only time in his entire career that he could remember having cheated.

His final adventure in the world of rallying came at the end of the year when he rejoined the Rootes team for the Great American Rally, starting and ending in New York and going up through New England to the Canadian border. As they tackled the snow-covered Lincoln Gap, a mountain pass in Vermont, Moss complained that, because he couldn't get his Sunbeam to the top, the stage should be cancelled. When a rival pointed to a set of tyre tracks which indicated that the official car had managed it, the Englishman's objection was drowned in the sound of other competitors restarting their engines and setting off to tackle the climb. A squad of Oldsmobiles won both the overall victory and the team prize.

Consolation for that inglorious finale to his rallying career came before he set off for home, in a message telling him that he was about to become a Mercedes-Benz Grand Prix driver.

After their two Mercedes finish a length apart in the 1955 British Grand Prix, Juan Manuel Fangio congratulates Moss on his first win in a world championship race (George Phillips/Revs Institute).

# CHAPTER 26

# THREE-POINTED STAR

What would it mean for an Englishman to drive a Mercedes, only ten years after the end of a war that had killed so many millions? In 1937 Dick Seaman had signed up for the same team and watched as the shadow of war fell across Europe. He stood to attention when Adolf Hitler inspected the cars and their drivers in Berlin and made a reluctant Nazi salute on the victory podium at the Nürburgring. He had been killed, while leading a Grand Prix in one of the Silver Arrows, only weeks before Britain and Germany went to war. Now former foes were expressing unstinted admiration of Germany's engineering prowess as applied to the science of motor racing – skills that had only recently been used to fashion Tiger tanks, V2 rockets and Messerschmitt engines. It was as if the two things had no connection.

Mercedes' tentative return in 1951 with pre-war cars in Argentina – not exactly a hostile environment – proved only that reviving obsolete machinery was not the way to go. It was followed in 1952 by the development of new sports coupés which secured first and second places at Le Mans and in the Carrera Panamericana. That was more like the old Mercedes, and the company's full-scale return to Grand Prix racing in 1954 saw them resuming the sort of dominance they had enjoyed between 1934 and 1939. For Moss, just as it had been for Seaman, the invitation to join this historic team was the greatest compliment that could be paid to a racing driver.

Having rejected his overture at the start of the previous season, Mercedes had seen enough to conclude that he now had the experience to go with his talent. Ken Gregory had paved the way with a visit to Stuttgart, where Alfred Neubauer had immediately made an offer of a staggering £28,000 for the season (about £700,000 today). Since that was roughly twice what Gregory would have asked for, in the expectation of being beaten down, he felt able to accept on the spot. For that sort of money, Stirling would certainly abide by a contractual obligation to be in bed by ten o'clock on the night before a race. Although the deal left him free to drive other cars outside the races for which Mercedes needed him, there would be no more messing around with rallies or picking up prize money in Formula 3. Gregory was soon setting up a company called Stirling Moss Ltd to handle his principal client's income and reduce the tax liability.

For his new team, the acquisition represented more than just the capture of an enormously gifted young driver: it also had a public-relations value. When Hitler endorsed Seaman's inclusion in a team whose successes were intended to proclaim the superiority of German technology, he was still hoping that his country and Britain might form an alliance. Bringing Moss into the squad could have been seen as a friendly gesture to a recent enemy. It was also a hand outstretched towards a potentially lucrative market for road cars bearing the same three-pointed star.

Before leaving for America in November, he had tested the new Ferrari F1 car in secret at Monza and visited Modena to talk to Omer Orsi. He had turned down Enzo Ferrari's offer, but Orsi had said goodbye to him believing that the arrangement with Maserati would continue into 1955. When Orsi learned that the man he expected to lead his team would be joining Mercedes, a telegram was sent to Stuttgart, warning them that Moss was already committed for the coming season. But although a contract was sitting on Moss's desk in London, it had not been signed. Jaguar's management was similarly disappointed, since the deal with Mercedes included driving the German cars in the major sports car races.

The news drew a mixed reaction in the British press, but most understood why Moss was following Hawthorn's lead in signing for a foreign team. 'If there is any blame to be laid,' an *Autosport* editorial declared, 'then it will fall on the British motor industry, who by their continued apathy to the importance of full-scale Grand Prix racing have virtually forced our best drivers to seek their fortunes with foreign products. In the case of Moss, the foreign country is one whose cars are presenting a real challenge to the British industry, judging by the number of cars now to be seen in England.'

In the final weeks of 1954 there was an invitation to a special Mercedes test session at Hockenheim, arranged just for Moss. He arrived with his father and his manager. A single-seater was ready and waiting, and one incident impressed him early on: when he came into the pits with his face covered in dust from the inboard front brakes, a mechanic was standing by with a bowl of hot water, a cake of soap and a towel. At Mercedes, he discovered, you could have anything you needed. Or they'd give you a good reason for refusing. 'If you asked for square wheels,' he told the journalist Maurice Hamilton, 'they'd look in the book and say, "We tried that in 1928 and they vibrated too much." They used four-spoke steering wheels, but I liked three-spoke, so that's what they made.'

He would also have noticed immediately that there was no sound quite like that of the Mercedes straight-eight engine. The noise was channeled through twin exhaust pipes curving outwards as they made their exit through the side of the bodywork just in front of the cockpit. Compared to the bellow of a four-cylinder Ferrari, the howl of a straight-six Maserati or the scream of a V8 Lancia, it was a fierce, unrelenting, leonine roar that seemed to swallow the air and shake the grandstands. It was loud beyond belief: a sound that engulfed the opposition.

These Silver Arrows were being run by the same duo who had supervised their pre-war successes: Neubauer, who had virtually invented the art of Grand Prix team management, and the designer and engineer Rudolf Uhlenhaut. Like Seaman, Moss got on well with both of them straight away. For all his fearsome reputation, Neubauer liked to dine well and had an engagingly boisterous sense of humour. Uhlenhaut had been born and spent his early years in London, where his father worked for the Deutsche Bank before the Great War. In testing, he could step into a car and put in laps that matched those of the team's drivers. Moss spoke no German, but Neubauer's English was serviceable and Uhlenhaut's was perfect.

With characteristic Mercedes thoroughness, the W196 was produced in short-, medium- and long-wheelbase configurations to suit individual circuits, and with dramatic fully streamlined bodies for use at high-speed tracks. It was a big car, unhandsome in a well-muscled way in its usual open-wheeled guise, quite heavy to drive and with an unusual arrangement in the footwell: the brake and the clutch pedals were separated by a very wide transmission housing, meaning that the driver's legs were splayed apart. Moss found that easier to get used to than the gearshift pattern, which had first, third and fifth at the back of the gate and second and fourth at the top. It could also be tricky to handle in the wet, and even in the dry it was not a car that could be flung about in the same way as a 250F. But the power and torque of its engine and its all-round sturdiness made it superior to anything Ferrari or Maserati could produce. At a price, of course: it was estimated that each W196 cost the company around £50,000 to build, about ten times what Maserati were asking their customers for a 250F.

Moss was engaged as Fangio's number two, a position he was happy to accept since it enabled him to spend a year following closely in the wheel tracks of the man he respected above all others, measuring his own performance by the best possible yardstick. This was his finishing school: a clear hierarchy of master and pupil (although, as the season progressed, Moss would note with interest that Fangio was often happy to accept his suggestions on gear ratios and other mechanical settings). The bond between the two men was strong: neither spoke the other's native language, so they conversed in basic Italian. Moss never wavered from his belief that Fangio, eighteen years his senior, was the greatest of them all.

Their first race as teammates was in front of Fangio's home fans, the temperature at the Buenos Aires autodrome topping 100 degrees at the start of the opening round of the 1955 world championship series. Fangio won, driving solo, but even he needed a pit stop lasting three minutes to cool himself down while drinking several litres of lemonade. As for Moss and his two other teammates, Hans Herrmann and Karl Kling, they made use of the rule allowing more than one driver to share a car. Moss was lying second, with Union Jack stickers on either side of his head fairing, as he had requested, and extra cooling vents cut into the body-work, when a vapour lock in the fuel system stopped the car out on the circuit; he parked it, got out and lay down on a shaded patch of grass, seemingly exhausted. Suddenly, before he could make himself understood, he was being whisked off to the medical centre. Finally succeeding in getting himself discharged, he returned to the pits. With the race still under way, and seeing that he was fit and ready to resume, Neubauer sent him out in a car that had already been driven by Herrmann and Kling; together they were able to finish fourth, splitting the three championship points between them, as the rules then permitted.

They met President Perón at an official reception for the team and paid a visit to the resort of Mar del Plata before returning to the track for the City of Buenos Aires Grand Prix. Held under Formula Libre rules, the race enabled Mercedes to try out the three-litre sports-car engines they had brought from Germany. It was run in two heats, the aggregate times determining the winner. Farina won the first in a Ferrari, followed by Fangio and Moss, who then pipped his team leader to victory in the second. Although Fangio's combined times gave him the overall victory, the Englishman had shown that he could compete on level terms.

At Monaco he started on the outside of the front row, alongside Fangio and Eugenio Castellotti's impressive new Lancia, outbraking them both into the Gasworks hairpin and squeezing his team leader towards the outside of the track on the exit before thinking better of it and tucking in behind. Both in new short-wheelbase cars, they looked set for a one–two victory until Fangio's transmission broke at half-distance. On a glorious day, watched by packed grandstands, Moss led for thirty laps until, to his surprise and dismay, his engine failed. He drew up alongside the pits before pushing the car across the line to be classified last of the nine finishers.

A more spectacular exit from the contest was made by Ascari, who had been about to inherit the lead when his Lancia flew off the road at the chicane and plunged into the harbour. A frogman fished him out, the rescue confirming a belief among drivers that the use of safety harnesses would only hamper their chances of escape. But it would be the great Italian's last race. Four days later, during a test session at Monza, he went out in the Ferrari sports car he was due to share with Castellotti in the Mille Miglia and died on an otherwise deserted track in a crash for which no explanation was ever found. Just as Moss's defection to the Germans had deflated Maserati, the death of their double world champion knocked the stuffing out of the Lancia team, whose cerise D50 had been looking a match for the silver W196.

The Mercedes hegemony was re-established with one–two wins for Fangio and Moss at Spa and Zandvoort, running in close order in both races. The two were separated by only three-tenths of a second at the end of the Dutch race, in which they lapped the entire field. This was very much the sort of dominance enjoyed by the team before the war, when the quality of their engineering and organisation had made them seem invincible. At Aintree in July, however, there was a twist to the narrative.

After five consecutive races at Silverstone since the inauguration of the world championship, the British Grand Prix was being held for the first time on the three-mile circuit laid out inside the Grand National steeplechase course, run clockwise – against the direction followed by the horses. Compared with the continental tracks it was flat, featureless and artificial, and lacked even the challenging high-speed corners of the best airfield circuits. Its only colourful features were the vast colonnaded grandstands and a few evocative names shared with the horse-racing track: Becher's Bend, the Melling Crossing. It was destined, however, to witness two events that won it a particular place in the history of British motor racing – and that of Stirling Moss.

The first came on 16 July 1955, the day on which Moss won his first world championship Grand Prix. He and Fangio had set the fastest times in practice, and Fangio led him off the line when the flag fell in front of a huge crowd. Within three laps Moss had gone past his team leader. When Fangio repassed him, he had to snatch the lead once more. But an adroit piece of work in lapping a backmarker under braking for a corner, forcing Fangio to fall back, allowed Moss to build a cushion; this was a trick he had learned from Villoresi at Monza a few years earlier, while trying to follow the Italian's Ferrari in his HWM.

When Neubauer put out signs telling them both to ease up, Fangio crept closer. As the two silver cars crossed the finish line Moss was barely a length ahead, leading a clean sweep of the first four places for Mercedes. His shirt stained with sweat, his face black with oil, he accepted the victor's laurel wreath and a kiss from the formidable Mrs Mirabel Topham, a former West End Gaiety Girl who had run Aintree since marrying its owner before the war. He had become the first British driver to win his home round of the world championship.

Moss always said that his teammate could have won the race with ease, had he been so minded. When questioned in later years, Fangio invariably called Moss a worthy winner. What was the truth? With only one round of the championship to go after Aintree, Fangio had already claimed his third world title. A win for the young English hero would be of great publicity value. A year earlier, Fangio's Mercedes had finished half a second behind the car of his German teammate Karl Kling at the AVUS track in the non-championship Berlin Grand Prix, a popular home win for a veteran driver who, by any measure, was not in Fangio's class. A conclusion might be drawn. But Fangio did nothing to suggest that either victory had been gift-wrapped. And Moss's capture of the point for fastest lap gave evidence of his speed on the day.

By the time they reached Monza, Mercedes had dropped a bombshell by informing their drivers that the team would be withdrawing from Formula 1 racing at the end of the season. They were told that the lavish and highly expensive project was being terminated in order to concentrate the resources of the experimental department on the development of their road cars. Meanwhile, Neubauer and Uhlenhaut threw everything they had at an attempt to win the last race of the world championship year.

Since the Italian Grand Prix was being run over a combination of Monza's traditional road circuit and the new banked oval, a test session was booked at the track, where comparisons were made between the various wheelbase lengths with both open-wheeled and streamlined bodywork. Two brand-new cars were built as a result of the tests, but by the time they returned for the race weekend the surface of the banked track had been smoothed out and a new solution was required.

Hasty modifications were made, and two more chassis were built up in Stuttgart almost overnight and sent down to Monza. The work was done so well that the Mercedes team were again holding the top four places, with Fangio and Moss followed by Kling and Piero Taruffi, a guest in the team, when a stone thrown up by Fangio's car smashed Moss's aeroscreen. It was replaced quickly, but his attempt to recover lost ground was thwarted when a piston failed. His career as Mercedes Grand Prix driver ended in the pits, alongside Kling, who had also retired, the pair looking on as Fangio let Taruffi close up to within half a second by the time they swept past the chequered flag, the German team giving the Italian crowd something to cheer.

After that the W196s were taken home and packed away, their work done and their place in motor-racing history secure. In 2013 one of them became the most expensive car ever bought at auction. Donated by the factory to the Donington museum, it was sold to raise funds and was knocked down to a winning bid of £19,601,500.

# CHAPTER 27

# FANGIO'S PILLS

A year before he joined Mercedes, a smiling Moss had appeared in a newspaper advertisement for a popular glucose drink: 'What do I drink to keep me going in a gruelling race? Why, Lucozade, of course!' But one of the things that impressed him about Fangio was that the Argentinian champion, although now in his mid-forties, still possessed a capacity for physical endurance acquired in the great transcontinental South American races of the 1940s and evident when he completed long races in temperatures that were bringing much younger drivers to the point of collapse.

During their year together the world champion shared with his teammate what Moss came to call 'Fangio's little pills'. They were probably something very like the Drinamyl tablets – half amphetamine and half barbiturate – given to Second World War bomber crews and known to have helped Winston Churchill through wartime crises. Whatever they were, when it came to endurance races, the gruelling marathon events of motor sport, they proved their value.

Undoubtedly the highlight of Moss's year with Mercedes – and, to some, the zenith of his career – was his victory in the Mille Miglia, the time trial around a thousand miles of ordinary Italian roads, inaugurated in 1927. When Moss first entered the race in 1951 he and his navigator, Frank Rainbow, had tried using a primitive intercom system and written notes. Four years later the procedure was to be refined, and Mercedes were happy to give him a prototype two-seater 300SLR for a week's reconnaissance. When he wrote it off, they replaced it with a roadgoing 300SL coupé. When that was also wrecked, in a collision with an army lorry, he was handed the keys to a 220 saloon with which to complete his revision of the course. This time he was to be partnered by Denis Jenkinson, the Continental Correspondent of *Motor Sport*, who in a previous incarnation had won a world championship as the sidecar partner to the motorcycle racer Eric Oliver.

During these thousand-mile study laps Jenkinson borrowed a suggestion from their American teammate John Fitch by taking detailed notes, which he transcribed onto a roll of paper 18 feet long. The roll was then wound onto a spindle inside a custom-made waterproof aluminium box with a Perspex window, allowing the navigator to scroll through the notes and give Moss precise hand signals indicating the salient features of the course – fast left-hander, slow right-hand hairpin, hump-back bridge, railway crossing, and so on – as they went along. They practised wheel-changing and, with the help of the racing team's mechanics, familiarised themselves with any simple mechanical problems they might have to deal with on the long stretches between the Mercedes pits set up in Ravenna, Pescara, Rome, Florence and Bologna, at roughly

250-kilometre intervals. Both accustomed to late nights in their normal lives, but knowing they would be starting the race at daybreak, they spent the week before the race getting used to going to bed early and rising before dawn.

Their car for the race was given the number 722, reflecting their starting time: twenty-two minutes past seven in the morning, making them among the last of the 521 starters, the slowest of which – including tiny Fiat 500s, Citroën 2CVs and Renault 4CVs – had set off first, leaving at one-minute intervals from nine o'clock the previous evening. In just over ten hours Moss and Jenkinson would cover almost a thousand miles of closed public roads from Brescia to Rome and back, taking in Verona, Ferrara, Ravenna, Rimini, Pescara, Rome, Siena, Florence, Bologna, Parma, Cremona and Mantua, crossing arid plains at 170mph and sliding around hairpins on the Radicofani, Futa and Raticosa passes, eight cylinders roaring as they sped past unprotected crowds in city centres and tiny villages, leaving cathedrals, castles and country churches in their rear-view mirrors.

The day was not without incident. Moss misjudged a bend in the centre of Padua, bouncing off the straw bales and allowing the pursuing Castellotti in his Ferrari to pass them. But the Italian was overdoing it and had destroyed his car before half-distance. Thereafter they were unchallenged by anything other than Moss's desire to complete the difficult 115km section through the Apennines from Florence to Bologna, taking in the Futa and Raticosa passes, in under an hour. Once that was accomplished, and they had come safely through the final fast, flat sections into Brescia, they were able to savour their triumph. After Jenkinson had caught his breath and washed the oil and dust from his face, he sat down that night with pen and paper to write a first-hand account of the adventure, rich in detail and emotion, which he put in an envelope and posted off to his magazine in London, creating an instant and enduring classic of sporting journalism.

Moss had become only the second non-Italian to win the race in its proper incarnation, after Rudolf Caracciola in 1931, also in a Mercedes. How should posterity rank his feat? Ascari, Castellotti and Taruffi each won the race – in 1954, 1956 and 1957 respectively – with no passenger alongside to give instructions on the hazards immediately ahead. Perhaps, as Italians, they enjoyed the benefit of greater familiarity with the roads of their home country, but their achievements were also extraordinary. And it might be remembered that Fangio, driving alone in 1955 in another 300SLR, finished in second place, thirty-two minutes behind Moss, despite experiencing engine problems as early as Pescara and running the final portion of the race on seven of the car's eight cylinders. Moss was also fortunate in that this was a rare edition of the Mille Miglia not to be affected by rain. On 1 May 1955, every one of the 992 miles was bone-dry. A year earlier, Ascari had faced terrible weather from start to finish.

Moss and Jenkinson would be unable to win it again. In 1956 rain came down hard from the start and they were lucky to escape when their Maserati 350S slid wide on the wet road, smashed through a stone wall and was prevented from tumbling down a 400ft drop only when its progress was arrested by a tree. A year later they were thwarted when the brake pedal on their Maserati 450S – a car with which they believed they could challenge their own record – snapped off when Moss tried to slow the car from 130mph only 8 miles out of

Brescia, forcing him to use all his skill in bringing the car safely to a halt. They had been racing for barely five minutes.

In that 1957 race the Spanish nobleman Alfonso de Portago and his navigator Ed Nelson were killed in their works Ferrari when a tyre burst at high speed as they approached the village of Guidizzolo, taking nine roadside spectators, including five children, with them. The wrath of motor racing's critics – particularly in the Vatican – erupted and the 30-year-old event disappeared from the calendar. 'The most dangerous race ever held,' Moss called it, 'but the most exhilarating to win.'

He had entered the Mille Miglia six times and finished only once, but his record of 10 hours 7 minutes and 48 seconds – at an average of 97.95mph – would stand in perpetuity. In 1995, the year before Jenkinson's death at the age of seventy-five, there were few dry eyes at Goodwood as the two men were reunited in the 300SLR bearing the number 722, buffed up and sent over from the Mercedes museum in Stuttgart for a run-out at the Festival of Speed. And so venerated was the 1955 victory that, many years later, exact replicas of Jenkinson's waterproof aluminium box, containing reproductions of his pace notes on a hand-wound roller, with a certificate of authenticity signed by Moss, were manufactured by Stirling Moss Ltd, in a limited edition, priced at £1,395 each.

# CHAPTER 28

# LE MANS

As he stood next to Pierre Levegh's coffin in the church of Saint-Honoré d'Eylau in central Paris, five days after a crash that had killed more than eighty spectators, Moss may have reflected on the reasons why he had never enjoyed the 24 Hours of Le Mans. Although the race attracted enormous worldwide attention, the need to drive at less than ten-tenths in order to preserve highly stressed machinery over such a long duration made it a bore. Equally tiresome were the hours between stints, when the co-driver was at the wheel. More pertinently this day, as he stood behind Fangio in the church, wearing a dark suit, white shirt and funeral tie in homage to a man who had been so briefly their teammate, their presence underlined the special factors that made the race inherently hazardous.

The catastrophe of 1955 had been made possible by the mix of cars, big and small, sharing the circuit, creating a danger compounded by the different levels of ability among more than a hundred drivers, from Grand Prix champions to inexperienced amateurs. You're travelling at a hundred and seventy in what amounts to a Formula 1 machine disguised as a sports car, coming up behind a little 750cc Panhard doing barely ninety, driven by someone you've never heard of, and you're about to overtake him in the braking zone at the end of the three-mile straight. Has he glanced in his mirrors before turning in? Does he even know you're there? And in the hours between nightfall and dawn it was worse. Those were the special dangers of Le Mans.

Even before the start in 1955 Moss had a collision during practice with a tiny French DB while leaving the pits on the narrow straight opposite the grandstands. Two people were knocked down: one of them was Jean Behra, who suffered a bang on the head and leg injuries that kept him out of the race.

But the 24 Hours was one of the year's most important events, in terms of publicity and commercial value, and he made sure he was ready for it. Some drivers took a light-hearted approach to the famous Le Mans start, which required them to run across the track and jump into their cars; not Moss, who had been a schoolboy athlete and prepared himself for the short sprint, as well as for the business of not wasting a second in opening and closing the door and firing up the engine. As a result, he was almost always away before the rest of the field, with a clear track ahead and the chance to build a cushion over pursuers who were sorting themselves out in a high-speed traffic jam. 'Those starts were very important,' he said. 'No one was going to hit you if you got away in front, whereas you can be back a few places and some other idiot will do something and suddenly you're in the middle of the accident.'

He raced there for the Jaguar team every year between 1951

and 1954. On the first occasion, in a brand-new C-type, on a shake-down run before official practice began, he discovered what it was like to do 140mph in regular traffic down the *route nationale* that would become the Mulsanne Straight a day later. The best performance of the four came in 1953, when he and his co-driver, Peter Walker, led from the start and were only relegated to second at the finish, behind another works C-type, by the several lengthy pit stops needed to clear what was eventually diagnosed as a blocked fuel filter.

In 1955 he and Fangio were on their way to victory in the Mercedes 300SLR, holding an untroubled two-lap lead with fourteen hours to go. But much earlier, only two and a half hours into the race, Levegh's sister car had crashed into the crowd opposite the pits, with terrible consequences. A wealthy 49-year-old French sportsman whose real name was Pierre Bouillin, Levegh had been invited to join the team in sentimental recognition of his celebrated near miss in 1952, when he tried to drive the entire race solo in his Talbot-Lago but missed a gear change – probably through exhaustion – and broke his engine while leading with only an hour to run, handing the victory to the German team. Now his dead body was one of many in the worst disaster in the history of motor racing.

As ambulances came and went opposite the pits, ferrying away the dead and injured, the race went on, statements over the public-address system skirting around the scale of the calamity in order to avoid a panic among the crowd of more than a quarter of a million, and keeping the entrances and exits open for the emergency services. But at two o'clock in the morning, after much discussion among the Mercedes directors, the order arrived from Stuttgart to withdraw. As soon as the cars and pit equipment had been packed into the team's lorries, all the personnel – management, drivers, mechanics, guests – left the circuit, the lorries heading for Stuttgart, the drivers towards the team's hotel in Alençon. At half past ten that morning, as the race went on to its conclusion, a memorial service for the dead began at the cathedral in Le Mans.

Moss felt strongly that the unilateral withdrawal was a mistake. What difference would it make? Nothing would bring the dead back; in half a century of motor racing, nothing had ever brought back a dead driver or spectator. And he and Fangio were on course for victory in a hugely important race that, as fate would have it, neither man would ever win. Hawthorn, whose entry into the pit lane in his works Jaguar D-type had begun the sequence of events leading up to the accident, went on to take the victory – along with his co-driver, Ivor Bueb – and was much criticised when newspaper photographs showed him smiling and drinking champagne as he sat on the car afterwards, accepting the congratulations.

He had not, of course, been impervious to the tragedy in which he had played a part, but this was motor racing in the 1950s, when a race was run to the finish and casualties were accepted as collateral damage. But no one had ever been required to find the correct reaction to a catastrophe on this scale.

Forensic attempts to establish a definitive cause of the accident, and to attach blame to one party or another, went on for decades. Hawthorn had overtaken Lance Macklin's Austin Healey as they came towards the pits, doing perhaps 150mph to the smaller car's 120. Then, having overtaken on the left of the narrow road, he cut across in front of the Austin Healey and slowed, using his car's powerful disc brakes, to enter the pit lane on the right. Macklin jammed on his less efficient drum brakes in response, skidded as his wheels locked and steered left to avoid hitting the rear of the Jaguar, which stopped safely at its pit. That put the Austin Healey in the path of Levegh, whose Mercedes, running at close to top speed, was launched off the back of the British car like a rocket from a ramp. It hit the bank, somersaulted in the air, came down on a concrete wall, disintegrated and exploded, its blazing components hurled through the crowd filling the enclosure on the other side of the wall, scything down men, women and children in their dozens.

At that moment Fangio was coming up behind Levegh. The accident occurred in front of him. He thought he glimpsed Levegh's raised hand, perhaps a warning to him; but with no time to slow down, he reacted instinctively to find his way through the chaos. He and Moss would race on through the evening and into the darkness, only to be told that their effort had been for nothing.

The disaster was not enough to dissuade Mercedes from continuing their campaign to win the 1955 world sports car championship. A week after the Formula 1 season had finished at Monza, Moss and Fitch won the Tourist Trophy at Dundrod. The American was required to complete only a handful of laps during a seven-hour race in which Moss demonstrated his speed on the wet and treacherous track, outpacing Fangio's sister car and Hawthorn's Jaguar, and leading home a Mercedes sweep of the top three positions. When a rear tyre burst on the winning 300SLR, damaging the bodywork, mechanics had to cut away the torn alloy, leaving a half-exposed wheel. Jaguar's attempt to protest saw their team manager, Lofty England, striding down to the Mercedes pit, only to be confronted by Neubauer, who took off his trilby and used it to shoo his rival away. When the race ended, three amateur drivers had been killed in crashes during the afternoon, bringing an end to the use of the Irish circuit for four-wheeled competition.

Success in the sports car championship now hung on the Targa Florio, the historic time trial around thirteen laps of a forty-five-mile circuit in Sicily's Madonie mountains. Short of drivers for the three-car team, Neubauer asked Moss to nominate a co-driver for a race that would last almost ten hours. He picked Peter Collins, who – as well as being a fellow client of his manager, Ken Gregory – was quick, reliable and easy to get on with.

Collins's speed was needed when, with the car going well, Moss ended his first stint by sliding on a wet verge, going off the road and ploughing through the scenery, coming to rest in a field below the track. The 300SLR's sturdy build and the willing assistance of a group of spectators enabled him to resume with little damage beyond ripped and dented bodywork. Collins took over for five laps at maximum effort, handing the car back to Moss for the final spell with a good lead which Moss held to the end. Their time was almost five minutes faster than that of Fangio and Kling in the second-placed car. And the winning of the championship marked the finish of Mercedes' involvement in top-line motor racing for many years to come.

Although Neubauer hinted at a hope that the sports car team would continue its activities in 1956, the directors decided otherwise. Moss had been involved in each of the 300SLR's victories in its title-winning year, cementing the Englishman's belief that, although Fangio was the undisputed master of open-wheeled racing, he had the great man's measure in cars with enclosed bodywork. But for the German company there was also the memory of eighty dead bodies lying on French soil.

In 1956 Moss returned to Le Mans to finish second again, this time in a works Aston Martin DB3S, co-driving with Collins, having swapped the lead several times with the eventual winners, Ron Flockhart and Ninian Sanderson in a D-type Jaguar. A year later he found himself driving a car he truly detested: an attempt to cloak a Maserati 450S in dramatic bodywork, drawn up at his behest by the English aerodynamicist Frank Costin, but so badly botched in its hurried execution by the coachbuilders at Zagato in Milan that its performance was severely compromised. Worse still, the fumes from the engine, rather than being expelled from the car, were finding their way into the driver's compartment, along with heat from the radiator. After four hours, before the sun had even set, and to the great relief of Moss and Harry Schell, his co-driver, the transmission broke. That car would never race again.

Sharing a beautiful Aston DBR1 with Jack Brabham in 1958, he led for the first two hours until the engine failed. A year later Aston Martin sent him out, as Jaguar once had, to set such a punishing pace that the rival Ferraris would be lured into destroying their engines in the effort to match his speed; his own blow-up was the seemingly inevitable price, but the dividend was a victory, the biggest in Aston Martin's history, for his teammates Roy Salvadori and Carroll Shelby.

He was absent from the 1960 race while recovering from an accident at Spa, and the following year, in what would be his last Le Mans, he and Graham Hill were holding third place in Rob Walker's Ferrari 250GT when their water boiled away and the engine seized. When his career was over, Le Mans would be one of the things he missed least.

# CHAPTER 29

# MOPEDS & MINIS

His love of beating the London traffic lay behind a lifelong fondness for miniaturised forms of transportation. In his home city, his machines for personal transportation were chosen not only because they were nippy but because they were economical on fuel, sometimes didn't qualify for road tax and could often be parked without payment – or used, in later years, without incurring London's congestion charge.

Some of them he was given, others he was promoting, one or two he bought. Over the decades they included the Hercules Grey Wolf, a motorised bicycle; the Trobike, a 95cc moped; the Vespa scooter he used at his holiday home in Nassau; the Triumph Tigress, another scooter; the three-wheeled 197cc Bond Minicar, whose virtues he extolled in a newspaper article in 1955; a Heinkel bubble car in which he drove Katie, his first wife, from London to Goodwood, a distance of 63 miles, in just over an hour and a half before the creation of a motorway; the BMW Isetta bubble car he overturned in central London with the manufacturer's representative sitting alongside him; a BSA/Triumph scooter he launched with the comedian Harry Secombe in 1959; a tiny NSU Prinz, given to his first wife when they separated; and the Renault Twizy, a two-seater electric car he was using late in his life.

'You don't have to go fast to get amusement,' he once said, explaining his liking for his Morris Minor and for the Standard 8 that replaced it, modified to take a hotted-up Standard 10 engine: it would do 85, he claimed, at least before Ken Gregory, his manager, crashed it. 'The sheer thing of doing 120, 150, 180 in a straight line isn't nearly as much exhilaration as going round a corner at 75. With these little cars I can have a lot of fun without being a great danger to the public. I don't drive very fast on the roads. I nip in and out of traffic.' He also nipped in and out of the magistrates' courts, allowing the popular press to relish the spectacle of the world's most famous racing driver being nabbed for minor infringements of the same road traffic regulations that applied to ordinary mortals.

In the early 1950s he acquired a big Jaguar Mk VII saloon; it was available for longer journeys, particularly between events on the Continent. He even used it to win races for saloon cars at Silverstone, delighting spectators as it rolled alarmingly on its soft suspension while drifting through fast corners.

Purists were surprised by his approval of automatic gearboxes. Could they not understand that a man who made several thousand gear changes during the course of a single Monaco Grand Prix might want a rest from the chore in other circumstances? 'My idea of a car for touring in America would be a Lincoln or a Caddy or something,' he told an interviewer in Nassau in 1956, 'with air conditioning and a radio and reclining seats and that sort of thing. I can't see any point in shifting gears. I like automatic gearboxes and servo brakes and electric windows. A very bad thing to say. But I get a lot of driving in cars where I have to double-declutch and shift gears and I have to put earplugs in and the wind is howling around. I reckon if you want to go from A to B, you might as well do it in great comfort.'

# CHAPTER 30

# TRIPLE TEST

It was at an end-of-the-season reception in Stuttgart that Moss was told of Mercedes' decision to make a complete withdrawal from racing. They had just presented him with the pin in the shape of the famous three-pointed star, made of silver and diamonds, that the firm traditionally gave to their Grand Prix winners. He was shocked by the news. Now he was at a loose end. Still wanting very badly to compete for Grand Prix wins in a British car, but also tempted by an offer to lead the Maserati team, he organised secret test days at Oulton Park and Silverstone in which he would try out the 1956 Formula 1 designs from Connaught, BRM – now no longer run by a trust but owned by Sir Alfred Owen, chairman of the biggest family-owned manufacturing business in Britain – and Vanwall, a team set up by another industrialist, Tony Vandervell.

He found the new BRM powerful but awkward in its handling. Although the Connaught was slower, it had just won at Syracuse in the hands of Tony Brooks, a young man taking time off from his dental studies to secure the first victory in a continental Grand Prix by a British driver in a British car since 1923. The quickest of the three cars was the Vanwall, and Moss was impressed by the team's professional approach; they had taken the trouble to invite him for two seat fittings at their factory before the test.

There were also conversations and meetings with a wealthy American named Tony Parravano, producing a story in the *Daily Mail* which claimed that Moss, Collins and Brooks had been signed up to drive for a new F1 outfit. The idea seemed to be that Parravano would subsidise the Maserati team, who were always looking for someone to pay for the cost of racing. Moss and Collins flew to Modena to test the latest version of the 250F and discuss the idea with Omer Orsi, the Maserati boss, and his would-be American backer.

Parravano, born in Naples in 1907, had emigrated to the US and made a fortune from building tract homes – what the British would call housing estates – in Southern California, profiting from the huge post-war demand. The source of his initial capital was never clear. In 1950 he got the motor-racing bug and started buying cars for professional drivers to race. Eventually he began spending time in Modena, becoming close to Ferrari and Maserati and buying cars from both to be shipped home and used by drivers such as Carroll Shelby, Phil Hill and Masten Gregory. By 1955 the two Italian manufacturers saw him as a very valuable customer – particularly Maserati, who had been promised half a million of his dollars to develop a car for the Indianapolis 500.

Moss was under pressure to make a decision. Should he take a chance on a British team, risking a repeat of the frustration of 1952 and 1953, or should he opt for Maserati, a team with experience of winning Grands Prix? The daily press and the motoring magazines fizzed with speculation. To help make up his mind, he took the unusual step of hosting a dinner at the Royal Automobile Club on Pall Mall for a group of leading British journalists from Fleet Street and the motoring press, inviting them to hear and discuss his thoughts and then vote on whether he should sign for a British team or opt for the Italians. It was an unconventional idea, but a clever one: it made the journalists feel they had a stake in a story that was attracting national interest.

'Money doesn't come into this,' he told them. 'Whatever you earn – here or abroad – the taxman takes.' Six of his listeners, including the representatives of the *Daily Mail*, the *Daily Express* and the *News of the World*, voted for the purely patriotic choice. Nine, including Harold Nockolds of *The Times*, Peter Garnier of *The Autocar* and Denis Jenkinson of *Motor Sport*, whose opinion probably counted for more with Moss than all the rest put together, went for the hard-headed option.

More offers were still coming in. Enzo Ferrari again let it be known that there was a place for Moss in his Scuderia. Jaguar made an impressive offer – £1,000 a race – for him to return to the sports car team alongside Hawthorn. Had he chosen to race for one of the British teams in Formula 1, that would have made good sense since none of them competed in the major sports car events, although the idea of Moss, at 5ft 5in, and Hawthorn, at 6ft 2in, sharing the car in an endurance event would probably have been a non-starter.

In early December the press received a statement from Alfred Moss, announcing his son's decision to join Maserati as the Italian team's number one driver for the 1956 season.

While Stirling and Ken Gregory were in Nassau, Alfred had travelled to Modena with a lawyer to negotiate a contract with Omer Orsi. He told the media of his son's belief that no British F1 team was yet ready to challenge the established foreign powers. 'Stirling would very much have liked to drive solely for Britain,' the statement read, 'but as he has decided that he cannot do so this year, he has insisted that he should be free to drive British cars in six of the major sports car events, and the Maserati company has agreed to release him for this purpose.'

Of Tony Parravano there was no mention. After the talks in Modena, the American had drifted out of the picture. A year later, under investigation for unpaid taxes in the US, he would flee to Mexico, attempting to take nine assorted Ferraris and Maseratis – not even half of his collection – with him; four of them got across the border. In 1960 he finally gave himself up and was ordered to appear in court to enter a plea for tax evasion. Three days before the hearing, he simply disappeared. He was never to be seen or heard of again.

Apart from its night life and the absence of currency restrictions, Nassau offered Moss the scope to refine his skills on water skis (Getty Images).

# CHAPTER 31

# NASSAU

'Nassau', the American journalist-turned-racing driver Denise McCluggage wrote, 'was a string of coloured lights across a tropical night. Nassau was the sharp blip of racing engines on a sun-drenched dock, the soft boiling-fudge speech of the Bahamians selling straw hats along Bay Street. Nassau was an umbrella-drink concoction of star-dipped nights, white sands, conch fritters, a sea rimmed in turquoise (and as clear as gasoline), and racing, racing, racing.'

On Moss's first visit, before there was any racing there at all, he fell in love with the place. He enjoyed it so much during the short visit at the end of 1953 that he returned a few weeks later, and paid regular visits in the following years. It was a place where he could polish his water-skiing skills and learn deep-sea diving. It was also part of the sterling area, a group of countries – mostly attached to the Commonwealth – which pegged their currency to the British pound, and within which there were no restrictions on how much cash could be taken in or out, a particular convenience in the days before the invention of credit cards.

The main town of New Providence island, Nassau had been founded in 1670 by British settlers who initially named it Charles Town, after their king. Fourteen years later it was burned to the ground and rebuilt under its new name. Occupied at various times by the Spanish and the French, in the eighteenth century it became the headquarters of more than a thousand pirates, including 'Calico Jack' Rackham and Edward 'Blackbeard' Teach, to whom its harbour offered a safe anchorage between raids on shipping throughout the Caribbean. Recaptured from the Spanish for the last time in 1783, it finally settled down under British colonial rule. The town gradually expanded and by the 1930s its pleasant climate in the months of the European winter was making it an alternative to the French Riviera.

On his second visit, in February 1954, Moss spent a fortnight at the British Colonial Hotel. In conversation with the people he met there, including the hotel's owner, Sir Sydney Oakes, and the holidaying English sports car manufacturer Donald Healey, talk turned to the possibility of staging a motor race on one of the island's airfields. The initial idea belonged to an energetic and volatile American, Sherman 'Red' Crise, who had made his money from filling stations and importing liquor from the Bahamas during Prohibition, and had promoted midget car racing in his native New Jersey before the war. A keen sailor and a frequent visitor to Nassau, he invited the English driver to take a look at the disused Windsor Field. Clearly the advice was positive, because, when Moss returned in February 1955, taking Ken Gregory with him, he was given reports of the first Nassau Speed Week, held three months earlier.

The newly created Bahamas Automobile Club was chaired by Crise, and its president was Oakes, who was also a member of the Nassau Development Board. Sir Sydney owed his hereditary title to his late father, Sir Harry Oakes, a gold-mining tycoon who had moved to Nassau in 1935 to escape Canadian taxes. For his investments in local infrastructure, including an airfield, a golf course, a country club and housing developments, and various philanthropic endeavours, he was granted a baronetcy by King George VI in 1939.

When he was murdered four years later, struck by a miner's pick, his corpse burned with insecticide and covered with feathers, Nassau became a focal point of international attention. The Duke of Windsor, formerly King Edward VIII, who had been appointed Governor of the Bahamas during the war in order to keep his pro-German sentiments at a safe distance from Europe, took charge of the investigation. One theory was that Sir Harry's resistance to attempts to build a casino on the island had displeased the mobster Meyer Lansky, but other possibilities emerged. In particular, suspicion fell on Count Alfred de Marigny, a French yachtsman who had eloped with Sir Harry's beautiful daughter, Nancy, making her his third wife two days after her eighteenth birthday in New York, where she was studying dance. De Marigny was arrested and tried, but acquitted after evidence emerged that he had been framed. The crime remains unsolved.

Even with a war going on, the scandal added a certain dark glamour to Nassau's reputation, which blossomed in peacetime. Sir Sydney, who succeeded to the baronetcy, was keen on the idea of a race meeting as a splashy start to the tourist season. He had married a strikingly good-looking and vivacious Danish woman, Greta Hartmann; the couple became a symbol of the resort's growing appeal to the international jet set.

As a sporting event, the Nassau Speed Week was a combination of Royal Ascot, the Henley Regatta and the pre-war Brooklands meetings, but with a much more informal atmosphere, even more social activity and a guarantee of better weather. 'We like to think it's fifty per cent racing and fifty per cent fun,' Red Crise told *Sports Illustrated*. Each year the event kicked off with a parade of the competing cars and drivers along Bay Street. Throughout the week the night life would be in full swing at the Pilot House Club, Dirty Dick's and Blackbeard's Tavern. At the prize-giving dinner, the trophies were presented by the Governor.

Among those drawn to this festival of speed were wealthy American sportsmen who had acquired the habit of buying European sports cars, either for themselves or for professional drivers to race. That first year saw Austin Healeys, Ferraris, MGs and Jaguar XK120s – one with a Confederate flag on the driver's door – shipped across the 150 miles of water from Miami to take part. As in succeeding editions, the competitors' travel and accommodation expenses were met by the Bahamian government. Alfonso de Portago and Masten Gregory were among the winners, both in Ferraris. Greta Oakes, at the wheel of an Austin Healey, finished fourth in a race for production cars, the only woman in a field of fourteen drivers.

When Moss returned in December, it was to take part himself. He was a member of the Nassau crowd now, watching fireworks from Red Crise's yacht, dining with Sir Sydney and Lady Greta, enjoying the nightly black-tie parties. Other drivers that year included Porfirio Rubirosa, the Dominican diplomat, polo player and playboy who had raced at Le Mans and Sebring and would die ten years later behind the wheel of a Ferrari at dawn in the Bois de Boulogne on his way home from a party; the New York fashion photographer Gleb Derujinsky, a friend of de Portago, whose Ferrari he rolled during a race without significant damage; and Isabelle Haskell, an American heiress and racing driver who would later help her husband, the Argentinian driver and entrepreneur Alejandro de Tomaso, to take control of Maserati. The two big races, the Governor's Trophy and the Bahamas Automobile Cup, were won by the Ferraris of de Portago and Phil Hill. Stirling took part in three events, all in an Austin Healey 100S, one of three entered by Donald Healey, completely outgunned by the bigger machinery.

In 1956 he took his parents and sister along for a Speed Week holiday. This time he was more suitably equipped, at the wheel of a Maserati 300S owned by Bill Lloyd, his co-driver at Sebring two years earlier. The car had to be patched up after Lloyd hit an oil drum during an earlier race, but Moss kept Gregory and de Portago behind him in the 200-mile Nassau Trophy. The forty starters included three Chevrolet Corvettes entered by the factory, an indication of the event's growing prestige. By now Sir Sydney and his wife were divorced, although they remained fixtures at the event and both took part in the minor races, while Greta drew admirers like moths to a scented candle, particularly among the visiting drivers.

For 1957 the Speed Week moved from the scruffy Windsor Field to a five-mile course laid out on the runways of the more modern Oakes Field. Moss was entered in a works Aston Martin DBR2: after finishing fourth in the Governor's Trophy, he lent the car to Ruth Levy for the Ladies' Race, only for her to roll and wreck it while battling with the Porsche of Denise McCluggage, who was wearing her signature polka-dot helmet.

Not wanting the spectators to be deprived of further chances to see their star attraction at work, the committee persuaded a Dutch amateur named Jan de Vroom not only to lend Moss his 3.5-litre Ferrari, but to have the central throttle pedal moved to the right overnight. Moss repaid the generosity with two wins, including the Nassau Trophy. Six years after the humiliation in Bari, these were his first-ever races in a car built by Enzo Ferrari.

De Vroom had raced the Ferrari at Le Mans that June. The car, and much else besides, had been paid for by his companion, Margaret Strong de Cuevas, a Rockefeller heiress married to a Chilean choreographer. In 1973, addicted to pills and low life, De Vroom was murdered in his New York apartment, his throat cut by two hustlers.

Now Moss had just about completed his own home in Nassau, a two-bedroomed house he called Blue Cloud. He designed it himself; among its features was a sunken bath. But he missed the 1958 Speed Week, having asked Red Crise for $2,000 in starting money in recognition of the fact that, since he now lived in Nassau, he would no longer be costing the organisers his travel and accommodation expenses. Crise's response was characteristically brusque: 'The Bahamas Automobile Club cannot, and will not, pay starting money. We don't need the name drivers. I would rather field a hundred second-rate cars than eighteen or twenty first-rate cars.'

The disagreement was smoothed over in time for Moss to return with the Aston in 1959, winning a third Nassau Trophy. In 1960 he took part in the only go-kart race of his career, finishing thirteenth, before winning the Nassau TT in Rob Walker's Ferrari 250GT. On his final competitive visit, in 1961, he repeated the win – same event, same car – but retired from the Nassau Trophy when the rear suspension of his Lotus 19 collapsed.

The Nassau Speed Week continued until 1966, after which it was decided that a much-needed restoration of the track would be too expensive to justify its survival. Perhaps, too, some of the social appeal of motor racing had started to fade as the playboys gave way to the professionals. Earlier that year, Sir Sydney had been killed when his Sunbeam Alpine crashed on the road between Lyford Cay and the airport. According to the *New York Times*, his car 'failed to make a highway curve and hit a pole'.

# CHAPTER 32

# THE WILD ONES

As the second half of the 1950s began, Mike Hawthorn and Peter Collins were Moss's two most prominent British rivals in Grand Prix racing. The pair were also best friends. They had a spontaneity about them that never seemed to be part of Moss's character. They were permanently up for a lark. If no excuse presented itself, they'd invent one. Fire-extinguisher fights in hotel corridors were not unknown. Meanwhile, Moss would be fretting about tyre pressures and negotiating his starting money. That, at any rate, was the image.

Hawthorn, the son of a former motorcycle racer who had set up as a garage owner in Farnham, Surrey, made an impact at the wheel of a Riley in 1951 and moved into Formula 2 with a Cooper-Bristol the following year, catching the eye with brilliant performances against formidable opposition. Suddenly the fame of this pipe-smoking, beer-drinking hell-raiser had begun to threaten that of Moss.

In 1952, the year when they were separated by a single point in the race for the BRDC's Gold Star, they went head-to-head in identical equipment just once. That was at the British Empire Trophy on the Isle of Man, when both were driving Frazer-Nash Le Mans sports cars. Moss's gremlins chose that day to strike in triplicate: problems with the car's ignition, fan belt and petrol pump forced him into retirement, while Hawthorn finished third with a broken exhaust. At the end of the season, Moss made a late comeback to snatch the Gold Star, but only by dint of amassing points through his many victories in Formula 3, in which his rival did not compete.

By 1953 the fast-rising Hawthorn was a member of Ferrari's Grand Prix squad and made history when he nosed ahead of Fangio's Maserati in a desperate sprint for the line at Reims. He was easily identified by his height, his blond hair and his racing uniform, which featured a bow tie and a British racing green windbreaker. Off duty, he favoured sports jackets and tweed caps, looking like the sort of chap you'd expect to find in a country pub. On the way home from Goodwood to Farnham he would stop off for a pint of light and bitter and a game of darts at the Bricklayers, the Coal Hole or the Spread Eagle in Midhurst or the Duke of Cumberland at nearby Henley, or perhaps all of them. 'My definition of a memorable party,' he once said, 'is one that I don't remember much about.' As a young Englishman who had inherited an open dislike of Germans from his parents' generation, he was said to be in the habit, during trips to race in Germany, of leaving a copy of *The Scourge of the Swastika*, Lord Russell's best-selling exposé of Nazi war crimes, on the parcel shelf of his car for passers-by to see.

Collins, whose father owned a garage in the West Midlands, had the looks of a young film star and an easy charm, and worked his way up through Formula 3. He and Hawthorn were quick to form a deep friendship: neither of them took life too seriously, and they were both immensely attractive to women. By 1957 they were together on Enzo Ferrari's payroll, along with two Italians, Eugenio Castellotti and Luigi Musso, and Fon de Portago, the Spanish marquis and Olympic bobsleigh competitor. Within barely two years, all five would be dead – four of them on the track, driving Ferraris, Hawthorn in a road accident in a Jaguar.

Moss was friendly enough with the two Englishmen. He shared their interest in girls, but not in drinking beer or practical jokes or staying up late the night before a race. 'Stirling's approach to motor racing is no doubt the right one,' Hawthorn once said, 'but mine is much more fun.' Moss's close male friendships were formed away from the circle of Grand Prix drivers; they included McDonald Hobley, the former actor and TV presenter of *Come Dancing*, and David Haynes, a motor trader from Kent who dabbled in racing. But the rivalry, although fierce, was mostly amiable. When Hawthorn came back to London for a kidney operation at the end of 1954, Moss visited him at Guy's Hospital. Both Collins and Hawthorn were among the squad of ushers at his wedding in 1957. In the summer of 1958 he gave Hawthorn a lift from Paris to Reims for the Grand Prix.

Of the two, he was closer to Collins. Having co-driven a Mercedes to victory in the 1955 Targa Florio, they were reunited as teammates in Aston Martin's sports cars the following year. After Moss had been introduced to an American actress named Louise King in Nassau during one of the Speed Weeks, he advised Collins to look her up while passing through Miami, where she was appearing on stage in *The*

*Seven Year Itch.* Collins and King, the daughter of a senior United Nations diplomat, met for a drink on a Monday evening in February 1957; the following Monday they were married.

For the newspapers and magazines, the three young aces were perfect material: their exploits on the track were matched by their availability to the paparazzi. But although Hawthorn, a more mercurial personality in and out of the cockpit, was affable enough on the surface, privately he left friends in no doubt that he didn't care for Moss. And there is a story from Reims in 1958.

One night during the French Grand Prix meeting the drivers and team personnel were gathered at their favourite bar in the town. Drink had been taken, and Hawthorn made a bet with Stuart Lewis-Evans, Moss's teammate, to see who could climb faster up a couple of trees in the courtyard. Off they went. Standing below them, one of their more illustrious colleagues suddenly felt liquid falling on him. Looking up, Stirling Moss heard a voice. 'I've always wanted to piss on you from a great height,' Hawthorn shouted.

# CHAPTER 33

# MAESTRO

Nello Ugolini had been the team manager of the Scuderia Ferrari in the 1930s, talent-spotted by Enzo Ferrari when he was assistant manager of Modena's football club, which Ferrari supported. Running the team's Alfa Romeos, he supervised some of Tazio Nuvolari's greatest triumphs. Vastly experienced and a highly sympathetic character, Ugolini had returned to Ferrari in 1952, watching over Alberto Ascari's two world titles and Hawthorn's historic win at Reims. 'Among the drivers Ugolini is looked upon as a wizard who has everything under control,' Hawthorn wrote later, 'and it is quite a normal thing to find drivers working for his biggest competitors going along to consult him about their practice times, because they know he will have timed them all and will produce the figures accurate to a tenth of a second long before the official times are announced. They say he can time every car in a race with one stopwatch and he has a capacity for unruffled concentration which enables him to keep track of everything that is happening to his own and his rivals' cars so that he can react at once as the situation develops.' In 1954 Ugolini tried to persuade Moss to join the Scuderia. Then he returned to Modena FC as a successful head coach, taking them to third place in Serie A. Now it was he, universally known as *Il Maestro*, who welcomed Stirling back to Maserati as the team's new number one driver for 1956.

The Modena factory was a place where Moss felt at home. The chief designer was the brilliant Giulio Alfieri, and Guerino Bertocchi was a head mechanic of the old school who took out all the cars – whether destined for racing or road use – to test them himself before placing them in other hands. By 1956 they had brought the 250F close to its evolutionary peak, and were also producing a series of excellent sports-racing cars.

For Moss, the first assignment of a full season as their designated team leader was a busy fortnight in Buenos Aires, where the Argentine Grand Prix kicked off the Formula 1 season. He led Fangio's Lancia-Ferrari in the early stages of the race, but his engine began to smoke and a piston failed. There was consolation when, in one of Maserati's three-litre sports cars, he beat the massed ranks of the Ferrari works team, led by Fangio, to win the Buenos Aires 1,000kms and then took the non-championship Buenos Aires Grand Prix in the 250F, again ahead of the reigning world champion.

Wins with a works 250F in the Glover Trophy at Goodwood and with his own car in the Aintree 200 gave his home supporters something to cheer about, followed by even bigger applause when he won the International Trophy at Silverstone in a Vanwall. Since Maserati had decided not to send a car, he was able to accept Tony Vandervell's offer of £1,500 for this one-off drive. He claimed pole position and, after a poor start, led the race from the second lap to the finish, outpacing the Lancia-Ferraris of Fangio and Collins in both practice and the race. It would be his only outing in the green car that season, but a marker for the future had been laid down.

The Maserati team had begun the year in something of a mess, but Ugolini had restored order by the time Moss rejoined them for the Monaco Grand Prix. He started from the middle of the front row, between the Lancia-Ferraris of Fangio and Castellotti, and was ahead of the pack by the time they came out of the first corner. While the others squabbled behind him, he drove with smooth authority to pull out a lead that was never challenged. It was his first victory in a world championship race on foreign soil, and a very convincing one. For all the encouraging success with the Vanwall at Silverstone, his decision to chase the world championship with a foreign team now seemed fully justified.

In Maserati's sports cars, he collected wins in the Nürburgring 1,000kms and the Bari Grand Prix. When the 300S he was sharing in Germany with Jean Behra failed early in the race, they were switched to the car of Harry Schell and Piero Taruffi and won after Moss had made up a minute on Fangio's Ferrari in the final twelve-lap stint. But in Formula 1, the middle of the season yielded nothing better than a second to Fangio's Lancia-Ferrari at the Nürburgring before the circus reached Monza for a finale in which Fangio, Moss, Collins and Jean Behra all had at least a statistical chance of winning the world championship.

That was one battle in prospect. Another was the Ferrari versus Maserati rivalry, on home ground. A third was the internal fight between the young Italian drivers of Enzo Ferrari's team. To the massed ranks of the factory teams – five Lancia-Ferraris, four Maseratis, three Vanwalls, three

Connaughts and three Gordinis – were added six private Maseratis: a field of twenty-four cars full of colour and contrast. And from the start, the narrative of the fifty-lap race lived up to its dramatic potential.

In front of a full house, on a track that had dried after morning rain, Eugenio Castellotti and Luigi Musso raced into the lead, duelling so fiercely that within five laps both had destroyed their tyres. Castellotti had managed only another four laps on a new set of tyres before one of them burst, sending him spinning into the infield and out of the race. De Portago had retired on the sixth lap after a burst tyre had damaged his suspension. The Lancia-Ferraris were on Englebert tyres, a Belgian make whose rubber clearly was inadequate for the job – at least when the young drivers were pushing them beyond their limits on a poor surface. On the eleventh lap Collins, too, came in to replace a burst tyre. A second weakness was revealed when Fangio, battling with Moss and the Vanwall of Harry Schell, had his steering break under the stresses imposed by the banking. He got out and sat on the pit counter, seemingly out of the championship battle, which now appeared to be in the hands of Moss, who had established a comfortable lead as the result of others' misfortunes and the durability of his team's Pirelli tyres. Schell had retired, as had Behra. But Fangio, it was remembered, needed only a single point to retain his title, and plans were being laid.

Castellotti returned to the race in Fangio's car, which had been fitted with a steering arm from de Portago's machine but was now too far back to be in with a chance of a points-scoring finish. Musso, having worked his way back up to second place, came in for fuel and tyres on the thirtieth lap and refused a demand from the team manager to hand over his car to the team's number one driver. The pride of Italy, or so his gesture seemed to say, was at stake. The pride of Argentina was no concern of his. Five laps later Collins, in third place, made a stop and gave a different answer to the same request. He hopped out, Fangio hopped in. Whatever points they won would be shared. Had Fangio remained out of the race and Moss failed to finish in the points, Collins would have become Britain's first world champion. But the etiquette of the *droit de seigneur*, and sheer respect for Fangio's standing in the sport, were uppermost in his mind. It was a decision challenged only by the correspondent of the *Sunday Express*, who voiced the firm opinion that he should have followed Musso's example, sat tight and won for Britain. Others understood the meaning of his gesture and told themselves that, at twenty-five, Collins had plenty of time.

But there was drama still to come. Five laps from the end, Moss ran out of fuel. The car was travelling at speed on the long straight leading to the last corner of the road circuit when the engine died, but he would not have enough momentum to coast all the way to the pits. Up behind him came Luigi Piotti, in a privately entered Maserati. Quickly appreciating the situation, the Italian slowed down and, with the nose of his car against the tail of Moss's 250F, shunted the silent car towards the pits. After a few gallons of petrol had been urgently splashed into the tank, Moss howled back into the race, still with a good lead over Musso and Fangio.

During the pit stop Ugolini had warned Moss that his left rear tyre was now bald. Nevertheless he had set a new lap record, securing the extra point for the fastest lap of the race, before the sign came out to slow him down, just as a steering arm on Musso's car was breaking and sending the

Lancia–Ferrari careering across the track from the end of the banking to finish up against the pit counter, its shaken driver led quickly away. Now Fangio was on the hunt, cutting the Maserati's lead from twenty seconds to six as Moss nursed his tyres, but the margin was enough to secure the Englishman his second Grand Prix victory of the season. Three points each from the shared second place for Fangio and Collins gave the Argentinian master his fourth world title, while Moss's nine points secured him the runner-up position for the second year in a row, with Collins third.

He finished his year with the Italian team by travelling to Australia, where a non-championship Grand Prix was being held at the Albert Park track in Melbourne to coincide with the Olympic Games. No medals were on offer, but Moss dominated the race in his 250F against mostly local opposition – and won both the sports car races held on adjacent weekends in one of the team's three-litre cars. Of the seven cars Maserati had taken to Australia, three were sold to private local buyers before the team left for home. That was one method by which they subsidised their racing, as well as clearing their inventory in preparation for a new season.

A different destiny awaited Moss's Monza-winning 250F. It had already passed into the hands of Tony Parravano, who shipped it back to the US and then took it with him when he fled to Mexico to escape the tax authorities, part of his fleet of fugitive racing machines.

Married less than a year, Katie Moss displays the anxiety of the racing driver's wife as she watches Stirling from the pits at Silverstone in 1958 (Michael Ward).

# CHAPTER 34

# KATIE

They had met, briefly, during an early visit to Nassau, in 1954, when he was taking a few days' holiday on his way back from winning at Sebring. They were both water-skiing; she was staying with an aunt and working at the local theatre. She was eighteen years old then, and he was twenty-four. Two years later he was at Le Mans, racing with Aston Martin, when he spotted her on the other side of the track. He waved to her: 'Come over here!' She signalled that she lacked the necessary pass. He pointed to his competitors' armband. It would be all right. And it was.

She was Katie Molson, a member of one of Canada's most prominent families, with interests in breweries, railroads and banking. Of all the girls he had spent time with, in and out of the spotlight, she was the one. Her looks were not those of the beauty queens and the showgirls. There was no fur stole, no white gloves, no plunging cleavage, no blonde waves. She wore very little makeup. Had she been a movie actress, it would have been one of the more interesting ones — a

Pier Angeli, a Jean Seberg, a Leslie Caron. She was slender and neat-featured, her dark hair cut short. Her eyes slanted slightly downwards, lending her an air of thoughtful appraisal and perhaps concealed amusement even when the flashbulbs were popping in her face, the look of someone balancing the value of putting up with it against the desire to disappear.

After Le Mans, they were together almost straight away. 'She was a tomboy on the one hand and a lady on the other and sexy in both roles,' he told Ken Purdy. 'She was most adaptable; she was a good cook, she was a very good driver. We enjoyed a lot of things together. Katie's taste was different from mine and she was strong enough, if you like, to change my taste in many things, in the way I dress and so on.'

That Christmas he flew to Montreal, where she was with her family. They talked about marriage before going on to Nassau. After she had returned home, he wrote a note in his diary suggesting the depth and complexity of their relationship: 'I really am very much in love with K but it won't be easy; I make her miserable and she does the same for me; is it insecurity?' But she went with him to some of the races in the summer of 1957, pictured smelling a rose he was handing her across a restaurant table before the Mille Miglia, planting a kiss on his head as he sat in the Vanwall's cockpit, and in a happy group at Le Mans including the drivers Maurice Trintignant and Jo Bonnier in the days when the racers and their partners were friends together, sharing their experiences as they travelled the world.

They announced their engagement in July (with a specially posed picture on the cover of *Illustrated* magazine), and on 7 October, a Monday, they were married at St Peter's Church, Eaton Square, attended by TV news crews and Fleet Street photographers, with Ken Gregory as best man and Stirling's sister, Pat, completing a trio of bridesmaids with his secretary, Judy Noot, and Katie's friend Margot Beaubien. The ushers included Collins, Hawthorn, McDonald Hobley, David Haynes and the rally driver Peter Jopp. Other drivers were present, including Tony Brooks, Archie Scott-Brown, Duncan Hamilton and Jack Brabham. The couple left the church in a blizzard of confetti and a storm of flashbulbs. After a wedding breakfast for 600 guests at the Savoy, they spent the night in the Harlequin suite at the Dorchester and left the next day for a short honeymoon at the Amstel Hotel in Amsterdam, where their room was filled with flowers.

In a rather unorthodox conclusion to a honeymoon they were back in London a week later for Stirling – accompanied by his new wife – to adjudicate at the Miss World contest once again, on a panel including the actor Trevor Howard and the dress designer Norman Hartnell ('Judging bloody awful! Miss Finland 1st. Not in my first six'), before setting up home in his existing flat in Barons Court. Two days later, after he had tested an Aston Martin at Silverstone, they went to see Judy Garland at the Dominion Theatre and dined afterwards with the singer and her husband at the Dorchester. In November they were in Caracas, where all four works Maserati sports cars, including his, were destroyed in a series of accidents. In December they were in Nassau, where he won the big race at the Speed Week and they worked on the plans for the house they were building.

She was with him in Buenos Aires in January 1958 when he won the first Grand Prix of the season: their post-race kiss gave the Argentinian sports magazine *Goles* the image for its front cover. She was with him in Havana in late February when Fangio, his teammate in the Maserati sports car squad, was kidnapped and held overnight by pro-Castro rebels. Two weeks later she was trespassing on the pages of his diary to scribble 'Katie loves you more today!' At the Targa Florio, he took her for a lap in his Aston, completing the forty-five-mile circuit through the Sicilian mountains only ten seconds slower than his best practice time in the official sessions, or so he said. She was not with him everywhere: after winning the Caen GP, he travelled up to Paris to meet her.

But the way their life together was punctuated by the death of one friend or rival after another – like that of Collins at the Nürburgring in August – gradually eroded her resilience. 'Stirling couldn't have the emotional involvement,' she reflected. 'He just moved on. It was just the next race. I couldn't do that.' You would make friends with the drivers and travel from race to race with them, she said, and one day you'd have breakfast with them in the morning and that evening they'd be gone. And she would be left with the job of comforting the wife or the girlfriend. Yet it was something they avoided discussing. 'All that had its effect on me. I couldn't take that life.'

She was finding married life difficult in other respects, too, from the trivial – Alfred Moss, who often travelled with them, disapproving of her liking for a glass of wine with dinner on the grounds of cost – to the more serious – Stirling not allowing her to employ a maid at their home, denying her a say in interior decoration and giving her an allowance while forbidding her to spend her own money – to the utterly dismaying experience of having her words distorted by the journalists who clustered around them everywhere they went. Once, on the way to meet Stirling in a downpour, she was delayed for a minute or two because she had been getting soaked and stopped to buy a cheap plastic mac, only to hear him object to what he saw as a waste of money.

Over the new year they travelled to New Zealand, where he won the Grand Prix, via Los Angeles, where they attended a Hollywood party filled with stars. Then came two weeks' skiing in Switzerland – Katie was an expert, as she was at water-skiing, fly fishing and skeet shooting – followed by a visit to Buckingham Palace for Stirling to receive his OBE from the Queen, who asked him the question to which everyone wanted an answer: had he decided which car he was going to drive in the coming season?

They were living in his old flat in Challoner Mansions, but he had begun the search for a site on which to build a new house. In April, Katie's appearance on television when he was the subject of *This Is Your Life* prefaced a season during which she was gradually less in evidence at his races. He took his pal David Haynes to Syracuse. Katie was with him at Monaco and Oporto and Nassau, but was not on the plane to South Africa, where he saw in the new year with a race at East London. They exchanged greetings by cable.

Soon after the start of 1960 the news leaked out that their marriage was over. He was distraught. 'She left me, I didn't leave her,' he said, many years later. 'I was very much in love with her.' For a long time, even after she had gone back to live in the place where they had first met, he believed that the marriage might be repaired. Eventually, as his distress eased, he accepted the finality of his loss and began seeing other women. As part of their settlement, he gave her the house in Nassau. After a while, they rebuilt a lasting friendship.

In 1964 she married an American artist, Don Seiler, with whom she lived in Miami and the Bahamas until their divorce in 1970. Kate Seiler, as she was thereafter known, became a patron of art and music in Nassau and worked with charities providing scholarships for young Bahamians. When a film crew arrived in Nassau to shoot scenes for the James Bond film *Thunderball* in 1965, it was she who shot the clay pigeons at which Sean Connery appeared to be aiming. In 2015 she returned to Montreal, where some of her time was spent serving food in a women's shelter. She died there of cancer on 17 April 2020 – three days after Stirling's death.

# CHAPTER 35

# MADE IN ACTON

Tony Vandervell offered Moss a retainer of £5,000, paid in monthly installments, plus a fee of £1,000 a race to lead his squad of Vanwalls in 1957. Out of that he would have to pay his own expenses, including travel and hotels. Thirty years older than Moss, Vandervell was used to driving a hard bargain; this would not be the cushioned five-star treatment the driver had received at Mercedes, but it put him behind the wheel of a British car that might be capable of winning Grand Prix races. And he respected his new team owner: 'He appeared a difficult and gruff man, but he was very kind and fair, deep down.'

Born in 1898, Vandervell had served as a young engineer in the Great War. Like Alfred Moss, he had raced and won at Brooklands, in a Talbot, and also competed on a Norton in the Isle of Man motorcycle TT. But most of his energies had gone into taking the reins of the company his father had founded, originally making electrical equipment for horse-drawn carriages. Its breakthrough came in the 1930s, when

Tony Vandervell acquired the British licence to an American patent for a revolutionary design of 'thin wall' engine bearings, which became widely adopted around the world. In a sign of his persistence, he travelled to Cleveland and slept for six nights in an outer office before securing the necessary approval. Manufactured in a handsome modern factory on Western Avenue in Acton, in west London, the bearings secured the company's prosperity.

Soon after the war, along with other representatives of British industry, Vandervell was persuaded by Raymond Mays to join the advisory board of the BRM project. Quickly frustrated by an evident lack of progress, he offered to buy the team a current Formula 1 car from Italy to get them started. Using the Board of Trade import licence granted to BRM, in 1949 he paid just over £5,000 for one of Ferrari's latest Formula 1 cars, which arrived in time to be entered in the British Grand Prix at Silverstone. Renamed the Thin Wall Special, the car performed poorly and was then stripped down and examined. Soon Vandervell was writing to Enzo Ferrari, pointing out its many shortcomings. Since Ferrari used Vandervell's bearings and knew of his qualifications as an engineer, this did not cause the explosion it might otherwise have done. He agreed to supply a new car, in exchange for the old one, for the 1950 season. This time Ferrari also sent Alberto Ascari to drive the car at the Silverstone International Trophy, but the result was no more impressive.

Communications between Acton and Maranello grew spikier. Nevertheless Ferrari sent a new engine for 1951, to be installed in the modified 1950 chassis, and at the International Trophy its driver, Reg Parnell, was leading the Alfa Romeos when a rainstorm halted the race and the Thin Wall Special was declared the winner. A win at Goodwood and a close second behind Farina's Alfa at Dundrod provided further encouragement for Vandervell to end his involvement with BRM and forge ahead with creating his own team, with a very clear ambition in mind.

'He was a sort of English version of Ferrari, or trying to be,' Moss said. 'He didn't like Ferrari, he didn't like what he called "the bloody red cars", but there's no doubt that he was very Ferrari-ish in his temperament. I suppose he was influenced by Ferrari, but he'd never admit it.'

It took Vandervell another half-dozen years to reach his goal, fielding a succession of good drivers – Farina, Collins, Hawthorn, Schell – in increasingly effective machinery. When he built a car, renamed the Vanwall, for the new 2.5-litre Formula 1 in 1954, its power unit was effectively four single-cylinder 500cc Norton motorcycling engines joined together in a design by the engineer Leo Kuzmicki. Having ridden a Norton competitively before the war, Vandervell had acquired an interest in the company.

He was putting together a team capable of taking a car that had begun life as an ugly duckling and turning it into a winner. Moss tried a Vanwall at Oulton Park in November 1955 and was impressed – although not quite enough to accept an offer to sign up for the following season. He put a toe in the water in 1956, however, when Maserati gave him permission to drive Vandervell's latest car in the non-championship International Trophy at Silverstone. By that time Colin Chapman, the brilliant young Lotus designer, and the aerodynamics expert Frank Costin had collaborated on modifications to the suspension and the bodywork that would bring the car to its peak.

The Costin bodywork had a strikingly smooth shape, resembling a wingless jet fighter, with a small oval opening in the streamlined nose and a high, rounded tail; its performance was even more impressive, not least because Vandervell had opted to use disc brakes on the car at a time when Ferrari and Maserati were sticking with old-fashioned drums. Moss put the car on pole at Silverstone and outpaced Fangio's Lancia-Ferrari, Hawthorn's BRM and Schell in a second Vanwall to take the victory. At Reims in July, after his Maserati retired early, he was able to watch Schell mixing it on equal terms with the Italians. Soon his mind would be made up. Omer Orsi's team had given him a good season, and he had finished second in the championship again, but it looked like Fangio was on his way back to Maserati and now he knew that at last there was a car in British racing green capable of competing for the title. And it would not be BRM, a team Hawthorn had left in mid-season, dismayed by its incompetence, or Connaught, which was in the process of going bust, with its assets up for auction.

At Vanwall the 27-year-old Moss was joined by two young men of great promise. Tony Brooks had abandoned his career as a dental surgeon in order to become a professional racing driver. A quiet and modest but determined 25-year-old, he had followed his victory for Connaught in the 1955 Syracuse GP with good performances for the Aston Martin sports car team, showing impressive speed in all conditions and on all kinds of circuit, although a Formula 1 season with BRM had proved highly unsatisfactory, not least when he escaped serious injury after the brakes failed at Silverstone and the car somersaulted before incinerating itself.

Stuart Lewis-Evans arrived in the middle of the season. A Kent-born driver with Welsh ancestry, he was twenty-seven and had come up through Formula 3. A congenital spinal problem and troublesome duodenal ulcers put his strength and stamina in question; like Brooks, however, he was quick enough on his day to keep the number-one driver on his toes. He also had a manager: a young second-hand car and motorbike dealer in Kent named Bernard Ecclestone, who had bought a couple of the Connaughts to run as a team but soon discovered they were too slow.

The early months of the 1957 season were full of so many disappointments that the Moss jinx seemed to have been transferred to his latest team. The car was fast – Moss set a new lap record at Syracuse and Brooks finished second to Fangio at Monaco in the opening weeks of the season – but unreliable. Although the engine delivered impressive horsepower, the drivers had to spend a long time persuading Vandervell, who considered his engineering knowledge superior to theirs, that it suffered from a serious flat spot. It took even longer to cure the problem. Vibration from the four-cylinder unit tended to break throttle linkages and fuel-injection pipes until fixes were made. But the biggest disappointment was not mechanical: it was Moss's crash at the Monaco chicane, when he led the race from the start but hit the barrier at the chicane on the fourth lap, taking the pursuing Ferraris of Hawthorn and Collins out of the race with him and breaking his nose, opening the way for a Fangio victory, with Brooks in pursuit.

Strangely, since it became so closely identified with his career, Moss was never a great fan of the Vanwall. 'It was no 250F, I'll tell you that,' he said. 'Aerodynamically it was pretty good, which helped at places like Monza, and the brakes were good, too. The engine was good, once they'd sorted out the dreadful flat spot, but the gearbox was very difficult to synchronise and in general, being a Colin Chapman design, the car was not user-friendly. Chapman's designs may have been the best, but they were not easy to use. They were not constant cars, that was the trouble. They were prone to both oversteer and understeer, and they'd just switch from one to the other. I don't know enough technically to be able to say how or why.'

Of course, he added, the car won races and eventually the constructors' championship, so it was perhaps unfair to make criticisms. 'It did what it was built for. But it was not a driver's car.'

Brooks agreed. 'The Vanwall was a car that didn't particularly like drifting. It was the complete opposite of a car like the 250F. Its basic tendency was to understeer. It was a very solid car in a mechanical sense, and you'd know where you were with it. But it wasn't forgiving in the sense that a 250F was. You had to be very precise to get the best out of it. Virtually everybody who tried it said the same thing.'

The gear change, he said, was 'heavy and ponderous, with a very long travel'. To prove it, at Monaco he returned to the pits at the end of the race, pulled off his left glove and showed Vandervell exactly what that second place had cost him: a bloodied palm worn raw by more than 2,500 of those heavy gear-changes over the 100 laps of the circuit around the houses, although it was later discovered that his car also had a broken clutch plate.

It was a different injury that cost Brooks a place in the team at the next grand prix, at Rouen-les-Essarts, and a non-championship race at Reims. During the 24 Hours of Le Mans he had crashed his Aston Martin into the sandbank at Tertre Rouge at three o'clock in the morning. The car overturned, trapping him underneath, and only a fortuitous sideswipe from a passing Porsche knocked the inverted Aston off him and allowed him to scramble clear. Severe cuts and bruises put him in hospital for four days before he was flown home.

Moss, too, missed the races at Rouen and Reims. After Le Mans, he and Katie had headed down to Juan-les-Pins on the Côte d'Azur, where they danced at a night club, gambled at the casino and water-skied. It was while practising a 360-degree turn on a mono-ski that seawater forced itself into his septum. The pain in his sinuses was so intense that injections were needed, followed by a trip back to Paris for hospital treatment that included lumbar punctures. Then came six nights at the London Clinic, where doctors drilled through his septum to release the trapped fluid, and then had to do it again. Eventually the pain receded enough to allow him to travel up to Aintree for the British Grand Prix.

At the two French races the cars had been driven by Lewis-Evans and Roy Salvadori. The latter shared Moss's ambivalent reaction to the car. 'It was very quick, quicker than anything I'd driven before. Nothing like the Maserati 250F that I'd driven previously, but it had lots of power. You were on top of the car, almost. And you just had this feeling that you had to be extra careful. It was too restrictive, as far as I was concerned. It needed a lot of precision. It told you who was the master straight away.'

For their home grand prix, Vanwall entered three cars, with Lewis-Evans joining Moss and Brooks. Their principal competition came from the four Lancia-Ferraris of Collins, Hawthorn, Musso and Trintignant and the four works

Maseratis of Fangio, Behra, Menditéguy and Schell. To the delight of the home fans, Moss took pole position, with Brooks sandwiched between Behra and Fangio on the four-car front row, and Lewis-Evans between Hawthorn and Schell in the second line as they prepared for ninety laps of the circuit.

Moss hared off into the lead, and stayed there unchallenged until the twenty-first lap, when his engine started to misfire and he came into the pits. But before the start, a deal had been made. Whereas Moss had recovered completely from his sinus problems, Brooks was still suffering from his Le Mans bruises and had lost a stone in weight from his slender frame, along with a great deal of physical strength. Foam-rubber padding had been added to his cockpit to reduce the pain from the inevitable buffeting. It was understood that if Moss had to retire, he would take over Brooks's car. And on the twenty-seventh lap the second car was duly summoned into the pits. Brooks, who had been lying sixth, was helped out of the high-sided cockpit, and Moss jumped in.

The lengthy changeover had cost another three places, but now Moss explored the limits of the car, the circuit and his own skill to hunt down his opponents. One by one they were overhauled: first Schell, who pulled in to retire, then Menditéguy on lap thirty-four, Fangio on lap thirty-five, Musso on lap forty, Collins on lap forty-six and Lewis-Evans on lap sixty-nine, putting Moss in third place behind Behra and Hawthorn. Meanwhile, an exhausted Brooks was sent out for a few laps in Moss's car, but its ignition problem proved beyond immediate repair.

The capacity crowd was enthralled by the chase, but even as their hero set new lap records it looked as though he was simply going to run out of time to challenge for victory.

But then luck took a hand and, for once, smiled on Stirling Moss. With twenty laps to go, and Behra seemingly on his way to winning his first world championship grand prix, the Frenchman's clutch disintegrated. As the shrapnel scattered across the track, Hawthorn ran over a piece of jagged metal that punctured his tyre, forcing him to limp back to the pits. Moss swept past, followed by Lewis-Evans.

There was still time for his surviving teammate to be hobbled by a broken throttle linkage, dropping him down to seventh, but Moss had enough in hand to make a precautionary stop for ten gallons of fuel before taking the chequered flag. Ecstatic spectators flooded onto the track and engulfed the Vanwall as Moss completed his lap of honour. On 20 July 1957, after years of frustration, they were able to acclaim the first victory in a world championship grand prix for a British car with a British driver.

Or British drivers, in this case. In the victory celebrations Moss was joined by an equally elated Brooks. The first prize of 2,500 guineas plus £500 for the first British car to finish would be divided according to how many laps each had driven: twenty-seven for Brooks and sixty-three for Moss. The eight championship points were shared equally; the rule permitting drivers to switch between cars was about to be removed from the regulations.

When I asked Brooks whether, given the rate of attrition among their rivals, he would have won the race had he stayed in the cockpit of his own Vanwall and seen it through, he replied: 'That's the $50,000 question. If only . . . As it transpired, it didn't require a flat-out effort to win. But that's with 20/20 hindsight. We didn't know how it would pan out. I never look back. Not in rancour, anyway.'

There were three rounds of the world championship left on the 1957 calendar. Nürburgring was a disaster for the Vanwalls, whose springs and shock absorbers could not be adjusted to suit the bumps of the fourteen-mile circuit. Buffeted by the constant vibration, Moss finished fifth and Brooks ninth, having been sick three times during the final lap. Fangio won, producing perhaps the greatest drive of his life at the age of forty-six to chase down and slice past Hawthorn and Collins after a long pit stop, securing his fifth world title in the process.

Pescara was a different story. Added to the calendar at the last minute, when fuel price rises following the previous year's Suez crisis led to the cancellation of championship rounds in Belgium and the Netherlands, the race started at breakfast time to take account of the extreme August heat. Brooks retired on the first lap with a broken piston and two laps later Lewis-Evans threw a tyre tread when he had just passed the pits, requiring him to drive an entire 15.99-mile lap at diminishing speed before he could get back to have it changed. As a result he finished fifth of the seven cars surviving at the end of a long morning's racing. Enzo Ferrari, who had vowed not to race in Italy again until he was officially exonerated from blame for de Portago's crash in the Mille Miglia, had finally given in to Musso's entreaties and sent a single car. But Moss won virtually without challenge, three minutes ahead of Fangio: another victory for a British car and driver, but this time on Italian soil. The rejoicing at the victory banquet that night was matched by the fireworks marking the Ferragosto holiday in the sky above the city.

The headlines and editorials were already being prepared by the British newspapers and magazines. 'In winning his second Grande Épreuve for Tony Vandervell in less than a month', *Autocar* would proclaim, 'Stirling Moss has placed Britain once and for all among the leaders in grand prix racing. It has taken four years of patient effort ... and now the rewards are coming in.'

Moss left afterwards for Rome, accompanied by his father in a rented Fiat 1100, heading for Fiumicino airport and a flight to London. Halfway there the head gasket blew, and he recorded in his diary that a taxi for the remaining 120km set them back 10,000 lire. They caught a flight at 4.10 a.m. and were in London by 8.15. Moss unpacked, repacked, collected Katie and her friend Margot, and set off again to catch a flight to the US, where he had an appointment with an MG in Utah. Later he would collect a cheque for £1,850 17s 6d for his efforts in Pescara, including a proportion of his retainer, starting and prize money and trade bonuses and minus the amounts advanced to pay the hotel bill for himself and his father.

He returned to Europe in time for the final round of the championship, at Monza, where the Vanwalls rubbed in their new superiority. The trio set the three fastest times in practice, with Lewis-Evans in pole position and Moss and Brooks alongside him in the brilliant sunshine. They were ahead of Fangio, who filled the fourth slot on the front row, and of the entire Ferrari team, now back to full strength. 'A truly wonderful sight,' Denis Jenkinson wrote in *Motor Sport*. Even more enthralling was the dicing in the opening laps between the three green cars and the Maseratis of Fangio and Behra, the quintet slipstreaming each other and going through the fast curves two and three abreast before misfortunes started to strike.

Of the Vanwalls, Brooks suffered from a sticking throttle, a gearbox oil leak and vapour lock in the fuel system, eventually finishing seventh, while a cracked cylinder head forced Lewis-Evans into retirement. But by half-distance Moss was almost a lap ahead of Fangio, his nearest pursuer, and that was how they stayed. As Moss came into the pits at the end of the lap of honour, his car was covered in a giant Union Jack. 'To beat the Italians at Monza is surely the greatest achievement ever made by a British racing car of any type,' Jenkinson wrote. Down in the Maserati pit, he reported, there was 'an air of bewilderment'.

Over the season, Vandervell's team had won three Grands Prix to Maserati's four. Moss had finished runner-up to Fangio in the drivers' championship for the third year in a row. The tide was turning.

# CHAPTER 36

# SALT FLATS

Speed records had been a big thing before the war, when the exploits of such Brooklands habitués as Henry Segrave, George Eyston, Malcolm Campbell and John Cobb made headlines. The world land speed record was on a par with the world heavyweight boxing title: everyone knew who held it. Schoolboys drew these aero-engined monsters – Segrave's Golden Arrow, Eyston's Speed of the Wind and Thunderbolt, Campbell's Bluebird and Cobb's Napier-Railton Special – in their sketch books.

In the immediate pre-war years the two big German teams, Mercedes and Auto Union, had hired a stretch of the Frankfurt–Darmstadt autobahn for a week in the winter to set new class records with their specially built streamlined cars, driven by the likes of Rudolf Caracciola and Bernd Rosemeyer for the greater glory of the Third Reich, which was paying most of their bills. Rosemeyer, the hero of all Germany, was killed during one of those events in 1938. The following year, on an autobahn near Dessau, the British driver

Major Goldie Gardner – who had lost the use of his right leg after being shot down on a reconnaissance mission in 1917 – drove his own highly developed MG to new records in the 1100cc and 1500cc classes.

Record breaking still had some appeal to the newspapers and their readers during the 1950s. Beginning with his 24-hour and seven-day exploits in a Jaguar XK120 at Montlhéry, Moss went on to attack records for 1100cc cars with a streamlined Lotus Eleven on Monza's banked oval in 1956, the day after winning the Italian Grand Prix. They had set 50-kilometre and 50-mile records at around 130mph when the bumps of the track fractured a rear chassis member and the back of the car fell off. Before that incident, Moss had appreciated the effectiveness of its slippery shape, drawn up by Frank Costin. The Lotus's Perspex bubble canopy and smoothly shaped body panels and undertray helped the car's passage through the air, while strategically placed vents kept the driver cool. It was this car which impressed Moss so much that he persuaded Maserati to invite Costin to design a special aerodynamic coupé for Le Mans in 1957, only for the job to be ruined by careless execution.

Two months after that debacle, Moss left Europe for America, and the Bonneville Salt Flats in Utah. In 1952 Goldie Gardner, then aged sixty-two, had set new marks in a new MG special, the EX-135, at Bonneville. Now Moss was heading there to undertake an attempt on the same records in a rear-engined MG called the EX-181.

A teardrop-shaped body with a small rear fin enclosed a supercharged, methanol-burning four-cylinder 1.5-litre engine based on those used in the British Motor Corporation's modest family saloons, the Morris Oxford and the Austin Cambridge, as well as the MGA sports car, already a success in the US market. On the nose of EX-181, a Union Jack and a Stars and Stripes were emblazoned together.

Moss was aiming at 240mph. That would be 60mph or so faster than he had driven before. Not such a huge gap, but the conditions were very different, both in and out of the vehicle. He would be lying on his back, guiding the car by means of an almost horizontal steering wheel as he made a timed run before turning to make a second run in the opposite direction, the average being taken from both. Before he set off, the mechanics would fasten the bodywork and the clear plastic canopy over him and close it with fasteners that would not be accessible from the inside. In front of him was an endless vista of pure white salt, the remains of a lake from the Pleistocene era, its crystals glinting in the clear air at 4,000ft above sea level.

It was a simple enough job, as long as he remembered to follow a strip of dark dye laid in a straight line down the course and not to destroy the special treadless tyres by accelerating too fast through the gears; as long as he could avoid being distracted by mirages appearing in the heat haze above the shimmering salt; as long as he could ignore the howl from the supercharged engine behind his head; and as long as he could overcome the loss of third gear on his second run.

After unexpected rain had forced them to hang around for two wasted days while the salt dried, the attempt was a success. Moss got the pretty little teardrop speeding over the endless white tablecloth fast enough to set world records for the mile, the kilometre, five miles, five kilometres and ten kilometres, all between 224 and 245mph. Then, slightly relieved to be out of that claustrophobic pod, he was on the plane and back home in time to be best man at Ken Gregory's wedding.

# CHAPTER 37

# KIDNAP IN HAVANA

While the racing engines revved, the small boy sat with his mother on a grass bank in the gardens of the Hotel Nacional de Cuba, taking in the noise and the colours: red cars, blue cars, white cars, lined up on the Malecón, Havana's seafront boulevard.

The city's finest hotel had been built in 1930 on the site of the Santa Clara Battery, two of whose artillery pieces remained as ornaments, pointing out into the Gulf of Mexico. Its guest book recorded the passage of countless figures from the world stage: Errol Flynn, Ernest Hemingway, Marlene Dietrich, Winston Churchill, Rocky Marciano, Marlon Brando, Frank Sinatra, Ava Gardner and the Duke and Duchess of Windsor. In 1946 it had hosted a Mafia summit convened by Meyer Lansky and the exiled Lucky Luciano. Sinatra provided the evening's entertainment as the mob bosses spent a week discussing how to develop their casino interests in Havana and Las Vegas.

Lansky now owned a piece of the Nacional, a gift from Fulgencio Batista, the President of Cuba. He and his North

American partners had enhanced the hotel's appeal to foreign visitors by adding the Casino Parisien nightclub, opened by the singer Eartha Kitt in 1956, its gambling facilities staffed by personnel brought in from Nevada. Within a couple of years the casino's takings were said to rival those of any Las Vegas establishment. A Grand Prix, with its aura of glamour and danger, was just the thing to lure more high rollers to Cuba.

And so here by the side of the sunsplashed boulevard, on Sunday, 23 February 1958, sat the young Philip Targett-Adams, better known a few years later as Phil Manzanera, the guitarist with Roxy Music, one of the most influential British rock groups of the 1970s. He was accompanied by his mother, who had appeared with her husband in a photograph in the previous day's newspaper, socialising at a pre-race function with Stirling Moss and his new wife and members of the staff of the British embassy.

'Obviously everyone was terribly excited because of Stirling Moss,' Manzanera says, looking at the newspaper cutting in his west London recording studio and imagining himself back in 1958, 'but my parents also knew all about Fangio – they'd lived in Argentina, where my brother was born. He and my sister were at boarding school in England. So I got plonked with my mother on the grassy knoll of the Hotel Nacional, and we watched the race – and it stayed with me. It was that wonderful and incredibly dangerous period – the drivers with flimsy little helmets and white overalls and the beautifully shaped cars, red and white and blue and black, and that amazing noise, so loud and exciting ...'

His father, Duncan Targett-Adams, had arrived in Havana with his family a few months earlier. As a young man he had joined the British Council and during his first posting, to the port of Barranquilla in Colombia, he met and married Magdalena Manzanera. Spells in Argentina and Uruguay were followed by a return to London, where he joined the staff of British South American Airways, with the job of opening up new routes.

In 1956, after that airline and others had been merged into the new British Overseas Airways Corporation, he was sent to Cuba to establish an office. In Havana, the family's temporary home was in the smart residential district of Vedado, in an apartment three streets away from the Nacional. They were installed in a permanent home, opposite the villa of Batista's Chief of Staff, by the time the weekend of the race came around.

The first Cuban Grand Prix had been held a year earlier over the same anti-clockwise 3.5-mile circuit. Starting on the northern carriageway of the Malecón, opposite the tall memorial to the 266 sailors killed in 1898 when the USS *Maine* was blown up in the incident that kicked off the Spanish-American War, the track passed the Nacional and circled the Parque Antonio Maceo before running back up the Malecón's southern carriageway, looping around the Parque José Martí along the Avenida de los Presidentes and returning down the Avenida Calzada to the finish line.

Slotted neatly into the calendar between the Formula 1 races in Buenos Aires and the Sebring 12 Hours, that 1957 race was quite a social event – the Hollywood actor Gary Cooper and his wife Veronica met the drivers in the pits, where Fon de Portago was accompanied by his new lover, the actress Linda Christian. The works Maseratis dominated the race: Moss led until his engine seized, leaving Fangio to take a popular victory. In a sign of political unrest behind the façade of an island presented as a paradise for gamblers and other pleasure-seekers, the European drivers were given bodyguards. Some of the drivers also attended the live sex shows that were a feature of Havana's night life under the joint dictatorship of Batista and Lansky.

A year later Fangio was back for the second Cuban Grand Prix, at the wheel of a Maserati entered by the Denver oil millionaire Temple Buell, and the world champion posed for photographs with Batista before the practice sessions. As for Moss, barely three months after racing a Ferrari for the first time, he was in another car from Maranello, this one entered by the North American Racing Team, Enzo Ferrari's US representatives. Moss and Fangio traded fastest laps in practice before a flimsy footbridge over the track collapsed, injuring several spectators. There was also a fatal accident to a local driver, Diego Veguillas.

By this time, anti-government guerrillas led by Fidel Castro were making serious headway in the fight to over-throw Batista. On the eve of the race, as Fangio chatted in the lobby of the Hotel Lincoln, a few blocks from the circuit, with Nello Ugolini, Guerino Bertocchi and Alejandro de Tomaso, he was approached by a bearded young man with a gun in his hand. Announcing himself as a member of the 26th of July Movement – one of Castro's revolutionaries, in other words – the intruder ordered Fangio to leave the hotel with him. A second gunman instructed other guests and staff in the lobby not to attempt to follow them and to do nothing for five minutes after their departure.

Two companions were waiting outside in a stolen Plymouth sedan. The group drove off with Fangio to the first of a series of safe houses in which he was held while the story flashed around the world, making newspaper headlines and leading TV and radio bulletins. According to Fangio's later testimony, he told the kidnappers not to carry out a plan to take Moss as well because the Englishman and his wife were on their honeymoon – not strictly true, but it seemed to be persuasive.

While Castro and his guerrilla army were fighting in the Sierra Maestra, the kidnap plot had been hatched by one of the 26th of July Movement's leaders, Faustino Pérez. Some of the hotel's staff, sympathetic to the insurgents, tipped them off about the timing of their target's arrival in the lobby. All efforts by Batista's police to track down the perpetrators and free their celebrity captive were to no avail. Meanwhile, Fangio, not merely unharmed by the ordeal, was making friends with his abductors.

One of them, Arnold Rodriguez Camps, told the Swedish journalist Fredrik af Petersens many years later, 'Our purpose was not to exchange him for money. We just wanted to prevent him from driving and to get maximum publicity for the revolution out of it – nothing else – and we certainly got it. We also wanted to ridicule Batista, and we did that in a big way. We needed to do something to show the world that we meant business but that we were not a bunch of murdering thugs, as Batista said we were. I am very proud of what we did and of the fact that Fangio was not harmed in any way. If that had happened, it would have been a catastrophe for us and the Revolution.' But the second Cuban Grand Prix had to take place without its principal attraction.

Manzanera and his mother were among a crowd estimated at 150,000 when the race started on the Sunday afternoon. In the early laps the lead was swapped between Moss and Masten Gregory in their Ferraris, but Roberto Mieres's Porsche had been dropping oil around the circuit and on the sixth lap a local driver, Armando García Cifuentes, lost control of his Ferrari at a kink on the Malecón, close to the US embassy, ploughing through the crowd before coming to rest against a construction crane. Seven spectators lay dead, forty were injured and García Cifuentes himself was driven to hospital by his teammate Abelardo Carreras, lying on the bonnet of another Ferrari, before being charged with manslaughter.

Gregory had been leading when he and Moss, in close pursuit, passed the scene of the crash, where a red flag was being shown to stop the race. But the wily Moss knew that the rules stipulated only the clerk of the course could show the red flag, and concluded that since the official was unlikely to have been where the accident took place, it was legitimate to carry on racing until they reached the finish line. Gregory, assuming the initial red flag meant the race was already over, reduced his pace, and Moss followed suit until, just 50 yards from the line, he dropped into second gear, floored the throttle and nipped ahead in time to be declared the winner. Afterwards a furious Gregory was placated by Moss's offer of 50 per cent of their joint winnings: prizes of $10,000 for first place and $7,000 for second meant that each of them would walk away with $8,500. With characteristic financial acuity, Moss told Gregory that if he were to lodge an appeal against the result, all the prize money would be withheld by the organisers pending a verdict – by which time Castro's revolutionaries might have taken over the country.

Fangio and his captors in their secret location listened to the radio commentary on a race that had lasted a mere thirteen minutes. That evening they watched the television news bulletins showing footage of the terrible crash. The next day, in order to avoid contact with the local authorities, he was released into the care of the Argentinian ambassador. Fangio made no subsequent effort to help the police identify the kidnappers. 'Although he could not have been very pleased,' Rodriguez said, 'he was a real gentleman.'

On his release, the world champion asked the Argentinian ambassador to let the news agencies know about it immediately: 'The lads [his kidnappers] had planted in my mind the idea that if Batista's people found me, they might kill me and accuse the movement of it.' A day or two later he left Havana and travelled to New York for an appearance on *The Ed Sullivan Show*. 'I had won the world championship five times and I had raced and won at Sebring,' he reflected, 'but what made me popular in the United States was the kidnap in Cuba.' Rodriguez and Pérez would eventually be captured, imprisoned and tortured by Batista's police; the former became a trade minister in Castro's government and would visit Fangio in Balcarce, his home town in Argentina.

The young Philip Targett-Adams returned to his school on the day after the race, sharing the excitement with his classmates. But that all-too-brief spectacle was nothing compared to the events that would unfold over the next ten months as Castro and his followers swept towards their date with destiny. On 31 December 1958 Batista stunned the crowd at a New Year party by announcing his decision to leave the country; he fled with forty friends and family members and hundreds of millions of dollars on a flight from a military airfield close to the Targett-Adams's home. The following day Phil and his family watched a gun battle between government guards and the *Fidelistas*: 'I remember machine guns, people screaming, my mother pressing my face down to the floor of the bathroom, bullets flying around everywhere, chaos, scary as hell.'

The new Castro-controlled Cuba hosted one final race, the Grand Prix of Freedom, in February 1960 – not along the Malecón but on a far less picturesque circuit laid out around the perimeter roads of Camp Columbia, the military airfield from which Batista had made his hasty getaway. The *Commandante en Jefe* attended a pre-race banquet. Moss was back, this time for his first race in Lucky Casner's 'Birdcage' Maserati, winning the 160-mile event ahead of the Ferrari of Pedro Rodriguez and Gregory's Porsche.

Phil Manzanera returned to Havana several times, visiting the landmarks of his childhood, including the grass bank where he sat with his mother on the hot weekend in 1958 when motor racing found itself caught up in events that helped shape the modern world. The impressions remain vivid. 'Cuba was dangerous and sexy then,' he says. 'Sex, drugs and mambo. And those drivers truly were heroes, weren't they? It really was life and death.'

The team manager Nello Ugolini (left, in cap) and the panel-beating artist Medardo Fantuzzi (right), creator of the Eldorado Maserati's bodywork, peer into the car's cockpit during practice for the Monza 500 race (Getty Images).

# CHAPTER 38

# THE ICE CREAM CAR

On the outskirts of Modena stands a cheese and dairy farm called the Azienda Hombre, making organic Parmigiano-Reggiano from its own herd of cows. It is also the location of a museum containing a priceless collection of road and racing Maseratis, including the unique machine that brought Moss close to death when its steering failed at 165mph on Monza's banked Pista di Alta Velocità.

The car is the so-called Eldorado Special, a 4.2-litre Maserati single-seater painted in the colours of an ice-cream manufacturer and built to compete in the 1958 Race of Two Worlds, which pitted the European teams against the Americans who raced at Indianapolis and the other oval speedways across the United States. The museum, a shrine to Maserati's history, was set up by Umberto Panini, a man who, with his brothers, made a fortune from humble football stickers. The tale of how these Maseratis came into Panini's possession is the story of the rise and fall of one of Italy's great car manufacturers.

Alfieri, Ettore and Ernesto Maserati constructed their first car in their Bologna workshop in 1926. Joined by two more brothers, Mario and Bindo, they were soon winning big races, including the victories in 1930 of Achille Varzi in the Coppa Acerbo and the Monza Grand Prix. In 1933 Giuseppe Campari won the French Grand Prix and Tazio Nuvolari took the Belgian Grand Prix. But the commercial side was rarely stable and in 1937 the Maserati brothers sold the company to the Modenese businessman Adolfo Orsi, signing an agreement to stay on for ten years and moving with him to Modena when he relocated the factory in 1940. At the end of the arrangement in 1947 they returned to Bologna, where they founded a new company. Prevented from using their own name, they built cars for racing under the name OSCA (Officine Specializzate Costruzione Automobili). The official, Orsi-owned Maserati team continued in Formula 1, and in 1957 Juan Manuel Fangio, enjoying a family atmosphere in strong contrast to the internal tensions that tended to prevail at the Scuderia Ferrari, became their first world champion.

The Eldorado Special was built for the second edition of the Race of Two Worlds. The first had taken place in 1957, when the Americans easily got the better of a token effort from the Europeans. Favouring the visitors was the use of the banked track, run in an anti-clockwise direction, like American ovals, and missing out the road section altogether. This suited the cars built specifically for Indianapolis, with two-speed gearboxes and offset chassis loaded for left turns only.

In the first year, a directive from the newly formed Union des Pilotes Professionels Internationaux – which some critics derided as a 'drivers' trade union' – led to an almost complete absence of top European drivers and teams to confront the ten cars and their drivers arriving from America. Having raced on the Monza banking, and believing that the event would be inherently unsafe, Moss, Fangio, Hawthorn and the rest were nowhere to be seen. Only Jean Behra broke ranks to represent the world of grand prix racing in a works F1 Maserati, but he withdrew after the first day's practice. Bizarrely, and probably attracted by the promise of unusually substantial rewards offered to all the finishers, the Scottish sports car team Ecurie Ecosse agreed to bump up the field by sending three D-type Jaguars, two of which had finished first and second at Le Mans the previous weekend.

Run in three heats, with the winner decided on the lowest aggregate time for the full distance, the race resulted in victory for Jimmy Bryan, from Phoenix, Arizona, who averaged more than 160mph over the 500 miles in his Dean Van Lines Special (named, like all the American cars, after its sponsor, in this case a California house removals company), making it the fastest race in history. He took away the Two Worlds Trophy and $35,000 in prize money, which was not as much as the $103,000 awarded to the winner at Indianapolis but still represented a very handsome reward by European standards.

In *Motor Sport*, Denis Jenkinson had fulminated against what he saw as the grand prix drivers' cowardice. 'If Fangio, Moss or any of the others have the courage to say point-blank, "I am too frightened to race on the Monza banking," then I will raise my soft-peaked cap to him for his honesty, but nothing more,' he wrote. 'To gather together behind the screen of an association is not only childish, it lacks guts ... Every year racing becomes more and more "milk and water" and real he-man motor racing is practically extinct, so that in the end one can foresee everyone wrapped in cotton wool, and then I hope they all choke to death in their own safety.'

Jenkinson's remarks provoked an outcry. A month later, writing in the aftermath of a race that he described as 'without doubt the event of the year', he clarified his feelings. He had not been casting doubt on the courage of Fangio, Moss and the others, but on the dwindling sense of adventure engendered by a Welfare State in which 'the tendency for the human being is to lead a safer and more secure life . . . I should have thought that the challenge to try a race that was faster and possibly more dangerous than anything yet run would have appealed to racing drivers, but apparently not . . .'

A year later, when the race was held for a second time, the Europeans – having seen that the 1957 event was run without accidents, and probably thinking of the prize money – tried to put on a better show. Ferrari sent two specially built cars for their squad of grand prix drivers, Ecurie Ecosse came up with a single-seater Lister-Jaguar, and Fangio and Trintignant were given drives in American cars. Maserati, having ended their official involvement in racing after their entire squad of sports cars was destroyed in Caracas seven months earlier, accepted money from Gino Zanetti, the owner of the Eldorado company, to construct a car based on Indianapolis principles – offset engine, two-speed box – and painted to resemble one of his ice-cream vans. It was designed by Giulio Alfieri, the father of the much-loved 250F, and Moss was persuaded to drive it.

In the two days of practice he indulged in a bit of psychological warfare against the visiting drivers. The weather on the first day was sunny. On the second day, however, a fine drizzle was falling. Back home, the Americans never ran in wet conditions; if it rained, the practice session or the race was postponed until the next dry day. Moss, being very used to racing in the rain, asked his mechanics to get the Eldorado Special warmed up. When the Americans told him that they wouldn't drive in such conditions, he pointed out that they would be making it much easier for him and the other Europeans to pick up the prize money. And then, to their amazement, he went out, circulating at a safe speed but making sure, every time he came past the pits, to give the car a burst of throttle to make it snake and weave in front of their impressed eyes as the big V8 engine bellowed out its defiant song.

To his friend and Mille Miglia co-driver Jenkinson, however, he had seemed apprehensive from the start of the weekend. 'It was a very frightened and nervous Moss,' the journalist wrote, 'who got into the big car and was pushed off into the pouring rain, but once under way he did his best to put aside all his inhibitions about track driving and turned some laps at about 145mph. Without exception the Americans raised their hats to the British driver, for the sight of the big white Maserati thundering down past the pits at nearly 160mph in the rain was awe-inspiring.'

Race day, as it happened, turned out fine. Once Luigi Musso, defending Italian honour in one of the Ferraris, had been overcome by methanol fumes after taking the lead in the first heat, the Californian driver Jim Rathmann, in the Zink Leader Card Special, won all three races and the prize for the overall victory. Moss was fourth in the first heat and fifth in the second. In the third, he was dicing with two Americans for second place in a manner that elicited Jenkinson's approval: 'Moss discovered that in track racing it was every man for himself. You did not move over and let your rival through. If he wanted to get by he had to find a way by and you raced as close as you could ... It was tough and rough, and the real Stirling Moss had suddenly realized that he could play it that way. The timid Moss of the pre-race days was pushed to one side ...'

Whether Moss's behaviour that weekend could truthfully have been described as timid, or whether Jenkinson was indulging in a retrospective justification of his accusations of the previous year, must remain moot. What happened next was that Moss had an accident which might easily have killed him. Four years later, when the BBC interviewer John Freeman asked whether he had ever thought he was about to die in a crash, he replied: 'Yes, I have. At Monza, my steering sheared at 165 on this banked track and my arms just shot around like this and the thing was out of control. I had virtually no brakes and I remember going up, hitting the top of the wall, closing my eyes, and then there was a whole hoo-hah and I don't know exactly what happened because I had my eyes closed. The car came to a standstill and I jumped out and there was a lot of dust and everything. I thought to myself, "If this is heaven, why is it so hot? And if it's hell, why is it so dusty?"'

In Jenkinson's words, 'A pale and shaken Moss got out, thankful for the retaining guardrail and for the solid build of the big Maserati, for a normal Grand Prix car would have fallen to pieces under the impact.'

Hoping to recoup his investment, Signor Zanetti had the repaired Eldorado Special painted black and sent it to Indianapolis the following year for another man to drive, Moss being otherwise engaged and thus denied a crack at a race he would never get a chance to tackle. Afterwards the car was returned to Maserati, hidden away among the company's collection of old racers until it re-emerged in confusing circumstances.

In 1968 the firm was sold by Orsi to Citroën. Seven years later it was put into liquidation and acquired for next to nothing by Alejandro de Tomaso, the Argentinian businessman and former racing driver, in partnership with a holding company owned by the Italian government. Eight hundred jobs had been saved, but the company continued to struggle until, in 1989, Fiat bought a stake. Four years later they took over the entire company, buying out de Tomaso and bringing the famous but perennially ailing marque under the umbrella of its old rival, Ferrari.

Better times lay ahead. But de Tomaso claimed that the company's collection of nineteen historic cars of all vintages had not been part of the deal, and after a considerable amount of legal argument they were returned to him. His immediate response was to send them to a London auction house, where they were to be sold as individual lots. But swift and concerted action by Italy's Minister for Cultural Heritage and the mayor of Modena brought an offer from Umberto Panini, followed by the safe return of the cars to home territory.

Among the beautifully preserved exhibits in the Azienda Hombre, the spectacular centrepiece is the Eldorado Special, restored to its original ice-cream white livery: not just a true one-off with a fascinating and somewhat lurid history but, for good or ill, the first car in top-line European motor racing to be branded and liveried with an outside sponsor's identity.

# CHAPTER 39

# A GAME OF BLUFF

'Pygmy car sent to Argentine for Moss' – the *News Chronicle* headline on Christmas Eve 1957 was looking ahead to the first race of the 1958 world championship season. The so-called 'pygmy car' was a two-litre Cooper-Climax owned by Rob Walker, who was becoming Moss's patron away from his works drive for Tony Vandervell's team. The Vanwalls were not ready for the trip to Buenos Aires: like the BRMs, which also stayed at home, their engines were being adjusted to meet new regulations requiring the use of something close to standard pump petrol rather than the exotic and specially blended alcohol-based mixtures previously employed in Grand Prix racing. But Moss could not afford to miss a round of the world championship, so he, Walker and their small group of mechanics, including Alf Francis, set off across the Atlantic to face the might of the Ferrari and Maserati teams, accepting the handicap of a humble four-cylinder engine increased from its usual 1.5-litre capacity but still half a litre smaller than the opposition, installed in what was basically a Formula 2 chassis.

Moss had another handicap: during what he described as a bout of 'fooling around' with his wife, one of Katie's fingernails had scratched the cornea of his eye. He turned up at the track wearing an eye patch to blot out his blurred vision, continuing to wear it beneath his tinted goggles.

To beat their opponents, including three of the impressive new Ferrari Dino 246 models for Collins, Hawthorn and Musso, the Walker team hatched a plan. Although they carried enough fuel to complete an eighty-lap race lasting two and a quarter hours, they had been told by Dunlop that a set of tyres would only last between thirty and forty laps in the high temperatures anticipated on race day. But pit stops would be costly for the team, given that the Cooper's wheels were secured by four bolts, as opposed to the knock-off hubs on the wheels of the Ferraris and Maseratis, which could be freed with a few blows of a copper hammer. So Moss went around on the eve of the race cheerfully informing his rivals that he had no hope of a win, given the need to make what would be a very slow stop – a matter of minutes longer than their own. He completed only three laps in practice, recording a time good enough for seventh place on the grid.

The race was to be run on a 2.4-mile circuit, the No. 2 layout at the Autódromo 17 de Octubre, built in a park to the south of Buenos Aires in 1952 at the wish of President Perón. The crowds had been moved back to a safe distance since the Argentine Grand Prix of 1953, the year in which Perón ordered that the public should be allowed in free; when a fan wandered onto the track, Nino Farina swerved to avoid him and lost control, his Ferrari killing a dozen spectators.

Moss was pleased to note that the day had turned out a little cooler than expected. Early in the race he worked himself up into fourth place, and then overtook Jean Behra's Maserati and Hawthorn's Ferrari, leaving only Fangio's Maserati ahead. When Fangio stopped for fuel at half-distance, Moss took the comfortable lead that none of his rivals expected to last. Soon Alf Francis was ostentatiously putting out fresh wheels and tyres while showing Moss signals to indicate a pit stop was imminent, with all the time penalty that implied.

With a quarter of the race left to run, the Cooper still had not stopped and the opposition began to worry. Musso, in the second-placed Ferrari, started to cut down Moss's lead, which had gone up to a minute. As the Italian hacked away at the margin, cutting it to half a minute with twenty laps to go, Moss could see his rear tyres wearing down. First the tread wore off, leaving them bald. Then he could see the white breaker strips that indicated the rubber was gone. He was now driving extremely carefully, trying to preserve what was left while maintaining a cushion to the pursuing Ferrari. Finally, the breaker strips wore away, leaving the exposed canvas carcass, which began to fray. When the chequered flag dropped, he was just under three seconds ahead of Musso. Almost unnoticed was the fact that he had driven half the race without a functioning clutch. The reports acclaimed a masterpiece of tactical bluffing, one that had given him an immediate lead in the world championship. As he and the Walker team celebrated, the Ferrari pit erupted in a storm of recriminations. They were, in Hawthorn's description, 'shattered'.

# CHAPTER 40

# THE TEAMMATE

When he joined Vanwall in 1957, Moss demanded the status of number one in his new team. Wholly focused on the challenge of winning the drivers' championship, he was intent on making sure that nothing, including his teammates, stood in his way. He had seen Fangio win his title in 1956 by collecting vital points when Collins gave up his car, along with his own chances, after Musso had declined to co-operate. That was the sort of privilege Moss wanted. David Yorke, Vandervell's team manager, was not a figure of authority comparable to Neubauer at Mercedes. Stirling could make his desires known, and they would be indulged.

Did he recognise that it would provoke resentment? 'To an extent,' he said. 'It was very difficult to exercise and it caused a lot of friction. If my car blew up, they had to give me another one. We had a good team, the strongest there was. I think Tony Brooks was the best unknown driver there ever was, if you know what I mean. I have great respect for his ability. He was very quick, as was Stuart Lewis-Evans. If you looked at the other teams, they had one driver who was bloody good and the others weren't close. We were all fairly close.'

Brooks knew the score from the moment he signed his Vanwall contract. 'The team spirit at Vanwall was very good, very strong,' he said, 'and Stirling was clearly the number one. He had the choice of cars and the choice of engines. The only thing was that David Yorke tended to limit my practice time, once I'd got a respectable time, because if I did a quicker time than Stirling, which did happen, Stirling would grind round until he'd beaten it. He'd try my car. Sometimes he'd have my chassis and his engine, or vice versa. I was messed about a bit in that respect, and it did make life difficult on occasion. I think I started the odd race in a car I hadn't actually driven in practice, and in those days there were big differences between the chassis. Today they're produced with such fine scientific precision that you get into a spare car and it's identical to your race car. Not so then, not at all.'

The reality of the arrangement became clear in their first world championship race as teammates, at Monaco. Moss crashed his car at the chicane during the opening practice session, bending the chassis. After repairs were made, he didn't like the way it was handling. So he tried the car allocated to Brooks, with his own engine hurriedly installed, and set a time that gave him a place on the front row. That was the car he raced.

The swapping went on at almost every meeting. In practice at Pescara he had a go in all four cars, including the spare. His own car was over-geared and the road-holding felt vague. Lewis-Evans' car had more satisfactory gearing but was suffering from a fuel-injection problem. Brooks's car, despite a tendency to overheat, was the fastest. Moss made his choice, and the distinctive white band was painted on its nose. Back in Monaco the following year he was doing the same thing, asking to have his engine removed and installed in Brooks's chassis because the front end of his own car had been juddering in the first session. For once, David Yorke refused.

'I think it was sometimes counter-productive,' Brooks reflected. 'When I was number one with Ferrari, I never took anyone else's car. I preferred to stay with the same car and really try to get it sorted and concentrate on getting a good lap time. The more you mess about, the more your objectives become non-focused.'

In 1958 Moss and Brooks were also teammates in Aston Martin's sports cars. Later Brooks discovered that Moss had asked for a lower gear ratio in his car and had been given it because, the management felt, he could be trusted to stick to the prescribed rev limits. 'They knew I could be trusted, too, but Stirling could call the shots with Aston as well as Vanwall.'

Nevertheless, he remembered, there was no falling out. 'I never had a cross word with Stirling because I knew he was entitled to do what he did. I never, ever complained because if I didn't like it, I shouldn't have signed on.'

Battling for the 1958 world title, Mike Hawthorn's Ferrari leads Moss's Vanwall in the opening laps of the Portuguese Grand Prix, with an outcome that would turn on an extraordinary display of sportsmanship (Bernard Cahier/Getty Images).

# CHAPTER 41

# CHIVALRY

In 1958 Moss had the best car – better than the ageing Maserati 250F and at least as good as Ferrari's new Dino 246 – and an excellent team. Fangio, now forty-seven, was obviously on the brink of retirement, which duly occurred when the five-times world champion quietly walked away after the French Grand Prix at Reims, where he finished a desultory fourth. His departure seemed to clear the way for the Englishman, who had finished second in the final standings for three years in succession.

By the time they got to Portugal in late August, for the ninth of the season's eleven races, he had won two Grands Prix, in Argentina and the Netherlands. So had Brooks, in Belgium and Germany. Hawthorn and Collins had won one apiece, in France and Britain respectively. But Collins, after a brilliant victory at Silverstone, had been killed at the Nürburgring, his Ferrari running off the road and tossing him out while he and Hawthorn were dicing with Brooks. Now Moss was starting every race as favourite, a status he confirmed on the streets and boulevards that formed the 4.5-mile circuit of Oporto, where the cars raced along an oceanside boulevard and across a square criss-crossed by tramlines in front of a crowd of 120,000 attending the country's first world championship Grand Prix.

His third victory of the season, and the eight points that went with it, was never in doubt. But sitting in second place was Hawthorn, almost a lap behind but ready to collect six points. He was also about to collect the single point awarded for the fastest lap, having beaten Moss's time. But Moss had been shown a signal from the Vanwall pit that he thought said 'HAW REG'. This triggered the memory of the sign Alfred Neubauer used to put out: 'RG', short for *Regulär* in German, *Regolare* in Italian or *Regular* in English and Spanish, an instruction that meant, 'Hold a steady pace'. He assumed it indicated that Hawthorn was not speeding up and offered no further threat. In fact, he had misread it. The sign said HAW REC – meaning that Hawthorn had set a new lap record, which would secure him the extra point. Believing himself had that point in the bag, and with a lead of two minutes and victory secure, Moss thought it unnecessary to speed up before taking the chequered flag.

On his lap of honour, he saw that Hawthorn's car had stopped in the escape road at a sharp left-hander halfway round the circuit. The Ferrari's drum brakes had been fading, and had finally been unable to slow the car in time to take the bend. Hawthorn had stalled the engine and was now out of the cockpit, trying to get going again by pushing the car in the direction of the circuit, as the rules permitted. But it was on a slight uphill incline, making the task impossible.

Moss stopped and shouted across, telling him to turn it round and fire it up by going downhill on the broad pavement. Hawthorn followed the advice and then continued, still in second place, to the finish. There, however, he was told by the race stewards that he was being disqualified for having push-started the car on the track against the direction of the race. As soon as Moss heard about it, he went straight to the officials and told them what he had seen. When Hawthorn restarted the car, he said, the Ferrari had been on the pavement – not on the track. So he had not broken the rules. After some discussion they accepted Moss's testimony and a grateful Hawthorn was reinstated that evening, along with his six points for second place and the one for the fastest lap.

In *Motor Sport*, Denis Jenkinson observed, with a hint of disapproval, that if Moss had just kept going and left Hawthorn to it, Stuart Lewis-Evans would have finished second, giving Vanwall their first one–two. But that gesture of chivalry towards a rival would have much greater consequences in the weeks ahead.

Hawthorn finished second again at Monza, the next race, this time behind Brooks. Moss had led from pole position, but his gearbox had broken. In Casablanca for the Moroccan Grand Prix, the last round of the series, Moss would need to win and make the fastest lap in order to take the championship, with Hawthorn finishing no higher than third. During the five-week gap between Monza and Casablanca, the tension rose as the newspapers made the most of the duel between the two men vying to become Britain's first world champion.

Moss did his bit in Morocco, leading without challenge from start to finish on the very fast circuit close to the sea, recording the fastest lap and finishing the race with nine points: a flawless performance. His teammates had hoped to help him by finishing ahead of the Ferraris, but both retired after accidents caused by engine failures. Hawthorn was sitting in third place until Phil Hill, the young American who had been drafted into the Italian team after Collins's death, slowed to let him through and get the result he needed to win the title by a single point.

So the title belonged to a driver who had won one grand prix in the season to Moss's four (and Brooks's three). Such was the peculiarity of the scoring system, which tended to reward consistency: eight points for a win, six for second, four for third, three for fourth, two for fifth and one for sixth meant that three second places were better than two wins. However distorted they seemed, the rules were the same for everyone. Hawthorn, Britain's first world champion, retired from the sport a few days later, his decision coming as a shock to everyone but himself. Collins's death had struck him hard, and he was coping with persistently debilitating kidney problems.

But the real tragedy that occurred amid the sand dunes of Casablanca's Ain Diab circuit was not the loss of a championship. It was the death of Lewis-Evans, who had crashed after his Vanwall's engine seized, the car sliding off the track and into a tree. The petrol tank ruptured, trapping the driver in a blazing car. After basic treatment at a local hospital, Lewis-Evans was put in the Vickers Viscount chartered by Vandervell for the trip to Morocco and flown back to England, where he was admitted to the specialist burns unit at East Grinstead Hospital. On the journey, Vandervell told his team manager, David Yorke, and his chief mechanic, Lofty England, that his enjoyment of the sport had gone. 'He wouldn't be lying in that stretcher if it wasn't for my bloody stupid hobby,' he said. After six days in hospital, Lewis-Evans died.

A month later, having just been asked, via a letter from Buckingham Palace, whether he would be prepared to accept the award of an OBE in the New Year Honours list, Moss was shocked by the news that Vandervell had decided to withdraw the Vanwalls from further immediate involvement in Grand Prix racing. In a reaction that would never have occurred to his greatest rival, whose entire being was bound up with motor racing, the English industrialist had been so profoundly affected by the loss of a promising and likeable young man in one of his cars that he no longer wished to continue. There would be a couple of token attempts to return in the following years, but they came to nothing. His heart had gone out of it.

'He didn't achieve what Ferrari had done,' Moss said. 'Let's face it, that was something quite different. He was gruff, certainly. I didn't mind him, I must say, because he was actually quite patriotic and I think the fact that he could make a green car that would beat the Italians gave him a tremendous kick.'

Moss had played his part, and he would go through the rest of his life without uttering a single word of regret over a decision that had made him the runner-up in the drivers' final standings for the fourth year in a row, and by the narrowest of margins: the closest he would ever come to the highest of honours.

# CHAPTER 42

# MELBOURNE

The crowd gathers around the helicopter, at a safe and respectful distance. Men and women, boys and girls, they are packed a dozen deep in a wide circle to watch the slight figure as he climbs aboard, still wearing his racing overalls, turning to give them a final smile and wave of his hand. The door closes, the rotor blades spin faster, and they applaud as the machine lifts off, carrying away the hero who has spent a magical day among them. Faces raised to the sky, they watch the helicopter hover briefly above the parkland, over the circuit where he has given them a glimpse of the deeds for which he has become famous, before he starts the journey back to his own world, many thousands of miles away.

This has been a typical day in the life of Stirling Moss, racing driver. It began, to the delight of the press photographers and newsreel cameramen assembled on the starting grid of the Melbourne Grand Prix, with a kiss from a film star – the English actress Sabrina (born Norma Sykes), noted for her hourglass figure and recently featured in *Blue Murder at St Trinian's*, in a role that required her only to sit in bed wearing a nightdress, reading a book. It has ended, like so many others before it, with a laurel wreath around his neck.

The date is 11 November 1958, and this victory marks the end of a season in which he has raced forty times, starting on 19 January in Buenos Aires and finishing here in Melbourne. He has raced in Argentina, Cuba, the United States, Great Britain, Italy, Monaco, the Netherlands, Germany, Belgium, France, Portugal, Sweden, Denmark, Morocco and Australia. He has avoided a kidnap attempt by Latin American revolutionaries and survived a terrifying accident at 165mph. Of those forty races, in eight makes of car, he has won twenty. He has missed being crowned champion of the world by a single point, the result of a gesture that will become almost as celebrated as any of his victories.

The helicopter is taking him to the airport, from where he will fly to the Bahamas. The next few weeks will be spent in Nassau, supervising the construction of a waterfront house of his own design. He and his wife will stay there until New Year's Day, when the papers report the news that he has been awarded an OBE. That day they take a flight to Los Angeles, where they attend a Hollywood party whose guests also include Tony Curtis, Gary Cooper, Joan Collins and Steve McQueen. From there they fly across the Pacific and back to the Antipodes, where a new season will begin with a win in the New Zealand Grand Prix.

The victory in Melbourne is the 143rd of his career. There will be sixty-nine more to come in the four years before the injuries from an unexplained and near-fatal crash force him to quit, still without the title that many believed to be his by right. 'If Stirling Moss had let his head rule his heart,' Enzo

Ferrari will write many years later, 'he would have won the world title he so richly deserved.' But today he is twenty-nine years old, close to the height of his powers and the apex of his fame.

# CHAPTER 43

# *THIS IS YOUR LIFE*

It's an evening in April 1959 and Eamonn Andrews, one of Britain's most prominent television personalities, is addressing the audience in the BBC Television Theatre. He's teasing them with clues about the identity of the subject of this week's edition of *This Is Your Life* – always a closely guarded secret until the moment Andrews, clutching the large red-covered book containing the biography in question, confronts the unsuspecting celebrity, who has been brought to the location of the live telecast under false pretences.

'He's a tricky character, this one – difficult to manoeuvre where we want him, when we want him – which is now,' Andrews says, addressing the audience sitting at home in front of their screens. 'So will you please come out into the street outside our theatre to see if we have manoeuvred him.' He is followed by a camera as he makes his way out of the theatre's main entrance and onto the pavement.

'We haven't got him here yet but there's a lot of traffic, a lot of people gathering in Shepherd's Bush Green . . . and let's hope that our man arrives . . . You do see the crowd gathering outside, even though we've hidden the name of the show tonight . . .'

A saloon car draws up, ordered into the kerb by a police-man on a motorcycle. 'Ah, this looks like trouble! Well, now, let's see – a speed cop, eh? Well, let me tell you, he's not a policeman at all – he's an actor. The people in the car don't know that, but we do.' As he speaks, a slightly built, balding man in a suit gets out of the front seat of the saloon.

'I've got a different sort of a summons,' Andrews tells him. 'Stirling Moss – there are the cameras – This Is Your Life.'

Moss looks surprised, turns as if to get back into the car, but then turns again and accepts Andrews' greeting. Together they walk through the small crowd and into the theatre before making their way down the aisle, Moss shielding his eyes against the spotlights, until they reach the stage, where several empty chairs are arrayed around a low table on which is placed a vase of flowers, with a TV set on a stand in the background. Andrews guides him into one of the chairs while positioning himself next to the TV.

'You know,' he tells Moss, 'we'd thought of putting a microphone in the car, but we'd heard of some of the things that you're alleged to have said to speed cops, so we thought we'd take the microphone out.'

'Just as well, actually,' Moss replies.

'Anyway, Stirling Moss, virtuoso of the steering wheel, This Is Your Life,' Andrews says, reading his script from the red-covered book. 'Now most of us only know you as a sort of robot in a racing car, remote and dedicated, come and gone in the wink of an eye. A young man in a hurry who knows where he's going – and usually gets there first. But that's today. Let's look at yesterday, or rather twenty-five years ago.' He turns to the TV set and the audience laugh as they're shown a blurry home movie of a child hurtling down a lane in a pedal car. 'Even then, a young man in a hurry,' Andrews says.

Two days before the programme, Moss had won the Syracuse Grand Prix. A photograph of a triumphant Moss comes up on the screen. 'This morning's headlines, there it was: "99 miles per hour – Stirling Moss does it again!" From boy to man, from obscurity to fame, from a bob a week pocket money to the salary of a prime minister – from start to finish, yours might be the story of one of your own racing engines: highly tuned, liable to blow up at times but the source of tremendous tireless energy.'

And now the story begins, told – as is the programme's tradition – by witnesses whose voices are heard before they make their way onto the stage. The first is a prep-school mistress, Peggy Shaw, who is there to tell us what a scamp he was. 'He had more than his share of energy and I soon realised that I had to have eyes in the back of my head. I used to say, "Whatever you're doing Moss, don't do it!" Touchingly, she produces a present he gave her when he was aged ten: a tiny bottle of Evening in Paris perfume. 'A fast mover, even then,' Andrews remarks archly.

We see film of the young Moss getting fit by hitting a punch bag before Andrews introduces the next guests. 'You might have spent your days saying, "Open wider, please,"' he says, and a disembodied male voice responds: 'And if I'd had my way, he would've.' It's Alfred Moss, who comes on stage accompanied by Stirling's mother, Aileen: a pair of proud middle-aged parents. They talk about his early racing career: 'He couldn't tell his mother or I that we didn't know what we were talking about,' Alfred says, 'because we did.' Aileen adds: 'The thing to make Stirling realise was that we did that for fun. We were amateurs. It cost us a lot of money. From a mother's point of view, I'd much rather he were pulling out teeth – it's much safer.'

Andrews describes how, when Moss got his hands on a Formula 3 Cooper in 1948, his first win came in a hill climb at Stanmer Park. 'That was the day we both got our names in the papers for the first time,' says the next disembodied voice, which turns out to belong to Lance Macklin, a smoothie in a regimental tie who has arrived from Paris to talk about how they had chased women together during their days in the HWM team.

Tommy Wisdom, the *Daily Herald*'s motoring correspondent, remembers the 1950 Dundrod TT, which Moss won in his XK120: 'I must say, Stirling, I liked your nerve, asking me if you could drive my car.' We see film of the following year's TT and hear the Spitfire-pilot voice of the BBC's Raymond Baxter: 'Two minutes ahead of anyone else, the chequered flag signalled another win for Stirling Moss, his second successive triumph in this race.' Ken Gregory, his friend and manager, comes on to speak of the disappointments of 1952 and 1953: 'Although we did our best and tried many things, at the last minute something always went wrong.' Gregory glances at Moss. 'I wish he'd learn to relax a bit,' he says. 'This is about the first time I haven't seen him doing anything. He's always designing a house or a car or a boat or something.'

Andrews summons the voice of an unseen Alf Francis. 'Hello, Stirling,' he says. 'I'm still catching up on the sleep I lost working for you.' Francis enters from the wings. Did he and Moss, Andrews asks, always see eye to eye? 'In the majority of cases, never! But then again whatever arguments we had, we just worked like two brothers. We could have been arguing but we were working to the same end.' He concludes: 'Since I came to work for him in 1951, I realised he was a champion. Now I think he is the greatest living.' 'Thank you, Alf,' Moss murmurs.

A piece of film from the Mercedes archive shows him with Denis Jenkinson in the 300SLR. 'Ahead of you now are the years of fulfilment,' Andrews says, 'the fulfilment for you of a special dream – to be first past the chequered flag driving not in the racing red of Italy or the silver of Germany but the dark green of Britain. At last, 1956, here it was, the Vanwall Special with you ...' – the audience applauds – '... as everyone knows, with you at the wheel, you were as good as if not better than the best. And 1957 brings with it another kind of success – marriage. After a hard day's driving – a wife to come home to, a chair to relax in.'

'Don't be silly, Eamonn. Stirling never relaxes.'

'That's the voice,' Andrews says, 'of his long-suffering wife, Katie Moss!'

And on she comes, cool and elegant, to hear Eamonn's scripted set-up: 'I believe that you're one of the greatest gin-rummy experts in Europe?'

'Well, Eamonn, if I'm not, then I should be. Because Stirling and I travel many thousands of miles each year in a plane and I usually like to sit and look out of the window or write letters, but he's always saying, "Well, come on, come on, let's play something" – gin-rummy or cribbage or something. He just never relaxes.'

'With all this travelling around, you must have watched him in a good many places ...'

'Yes, I have, but he changes when he gets onto the track. He becomes a different sort of person. He often doesn't recognise me. I know the times when I've stood in the pits and he's looked right by me.'

There's a slightly forced laugh from Andrews. 'But off the track he notices you, I bet.'

'He'd better.'

There's a hint of a smile. Only she and Stirling know that, after a year and a half of marriage to her racing driver, she is feeling the strain.

Then it's on to Paul Bates, a young man who caught polio and lost the use of his legs while doing his national service in Malaya. From his wheelchair, he thanks Stirling for the help he's given him: 'At fourteen I'd seen your first race, in the crowd, of course, and later at Goodwood it was one of the last things I did before I went to Malaya, only to come back like this. Your generosity helped so much to turn my dreams into reality. Several times you've been my chauffeur – some chauffeur! Seriously, though, I know it was your wish that your generosity should remain a secret, and I hope you'll forgive me for breaking my word.'

Juan Manuel Fangio is seen on the monitor screen, in a message from Rome, remembering the time they spent together – 'often as opponents, always as friends'. But Andrews has saved the biggest surprise for last.

'There is just one more voice for you to hear, Stirling, and it's a voice that you never expected to hear again. It dates back only twelve years but it's a reminder of the long, long way that you've come in that short time. I want you to think of yourself back in 1947: a grimy kid with a second-hand sports car and not much else except ambition. Sharing with you those long hours in your father's workshop, sweating to get it right, was a former German prisoner of war, a general handyman-turned-amateur mechanic. You know who it is, don't you?' Moss smiles and nods. 'That's right. We found him in Aschau, a little village in Bavaria – your first mechanic and your first fan, Don Müller.'

Müller comes on, a shy figure. 'I told him many times,' he says, 'I knew one of those days he would become one of the greatest racing drivers of the world.'

'You said it first, Don,' Andrews says, 'but today we're right with you. Stirling Moss OBE, This Is Your Life.'

The audience applauds, the guests gather round the star, and as the credits roll a continuity announcer's voice is heard: 'Actress Barbara Mullen from *Dr Finlay's Casebook* is the guest next week at the same time.'

Exploiting his interest in design and fondness for gadgets, Moss turned a former bomb site in a Mayfair side street into the epitome of contemporary urban living, frequently featured in newspapers and glossy magazines (RIBA).

# CHAPTER 44

# THE PAD

'My father taught me that if there was anything I wanted in life, I had to work for it,' Stirling Moss said. He remembered Alfred Moss reacting to being sent an early credit card by getting a pair of scissors and cutting it up. Out for a meal with a large group of friends, Stirling was likely to insist that the individual bills be apportioned according to exactly who had eaten what. His secretary, Valerie Pirie, remembered this happening with a party of twenty-eight at the Nürburgring: anyone else would have said, 'Oh, let's just divvy it up', but Moss insisted on going through it, item by item, to produce twenty-eight separate bills.

Perhaps the word was frugal. He was not ungenerous and he was not miserly. In the Luxembourg Grand Prix for 500cc cars in 1951, when he was only twenty-two, he had been so disappointed by the performance of his Kieft, which lasted a mere five slow laps, that he gave back his starting money to the organisers, less his expenses. But when his own money was at stake, he questioned the price of everything. 'I'm just not a wasteful person,' he said.

On a trip to race in Marseilles in 1951, one of his earliest forays into international racing, he discovered that he had been booked into the Hotel Bristol at 1,400 old francs a night, excluding breakfast – a couple of quid in those days. He crossed the road and found a more modest establishment charging less than half that amount. On his first visit to Los Angeles, he found the Beverly Wilshire Hotel too expensive and moved elsewhere. He cared enough about these savings to record them in his diary.

Soon he was among those high earners complaining about the level of income tax imposed by the British government. 'In my first big year of motor racing,' he told the London *Evening News* at the end of 1955, 'I earned £12,000. After tax, all I had left was £1,400. This year, I don't know. I don't know, frankly, what I have earned' – according to his manager, the Mercedes contract was for £28,000 a year – 'but as chairman and director of Stirling Moss Ltd I draw £2,000, on which I have to pay tax.' His best year as a driver, he would tell Doug Nye, was 1961, when he earned £32,500.

What his father also taught him was the enduring value of bricks and mortar. He bought his first property in Shepherd Market, at 36–38 Shepherd Street, in 1954, for £12,000, and set about converting it for use as an office. In 1961 he was scouting around for a place to build a new home from scratch in the same neighbourhood. The council invited him to pay £40,000 for a disused hotel and an adjacent bomb site at the top end of Shepherd Street. He declined the offer of the old hotel but bought the derelict site at No. 44–46 for £5,000. The original houses had been among five destroyed when a high-explosive bomb fell on the street at half past one in the morning on 16 November 1940, at the height of the London Blitz.

A casualty during the following year's raids was a nearby cottage, built in the early seventeenth century to house the resident herdsman who looked after the sheep brought to the ancient May Fair. The very particular history of this little bit of central London echoes through the words of the authorities who banned the annual fair in 1708, condemning 'riotous and tumultuous assembly ... in which many loose, idle and disordered persons did rendezvous, draw and allure young persons, servants and others to meet there and game and commit lewdness'. After Parliament had passed the Street Offences Act in 1959, the evidence of sexual commerce became less obvious. But the little warren of streets on the fringe of Mayfair still exuded raffishness, like an upmarket Soho.

Over the next few years Moss spent £25,000 building a six-storey house that became known, thanks to extensive coverage in television programmes and magazine features, as the ultimate bachelor pad – even when he was married. He employed an architect to execute his ideas, all of which were aimed at packing as much as possible into a relatively confined space, using imagination and technology. The features included walk-in wardrobes with motorised shutters, a spiral staircase, a lift, metal storage racks, heated lavatory seats, remote controls for blinds and entertainment systems and garage doors and buttons that enabled him to get a bath running at a set temperature from anywhere in the house, when such things were virtually unknown.

During his absences, the work was supervised by Val Pirie, who had barely left secretarial college and was already thinking of switching to a more interesting career on the day in 1958 when her agency sent her along to be interviewed for a job that would last eight years, establishing a friendship that continued until Moss's death. She kept his diary, sent flowers to his girlfriends, kept a bedside vigil after the worst of his accidents and eventually became a director of his company. More than that, she learned to adapt to the demanding and often disconcerting personality of a man whose well-known parsimony disguised a much warmer nature. No man is a hero to his PA, it could be said, and Pirie – whom he called 'Viper' – saw him more clearly than most.

Fifty years later he described 44–46 Shepherd Street as his best buy. 'Even if it were still a bomb site,' he told the *Daily Telegraph* with evident satisfaction, 'it would be worth £10m.'

# CHAPTER 45

# DARK BLUE

Stirling and Katie Moss were in Bangkok when they heard of Mike Hawthorn's death in a road accident on 22 January 1959. Having announced his retirement a few weeks earlier, the newly crowned world champion was planning marriage to his girlfriend, the English model Jean Haworth. He had been on his way to a business meeting in London in his heavily modified Jaguar 3.4 litre saloon when he came across Rob Walker in his Mercedes 300SL coupé on the Guildford Bypass. As could be the way of things in the days before the introduction of an overall speed limit, they started to race each other.

Some would later recall Hawthorn's description of his feelings about competing against the Mercedes team at Le Mans in 1955: 'I was momentarily mesmerised by the legend of Mercedes' superiority ... Then I came to my senses and thought, damn it, why should a German car beat a British car?' This was not Le Mans, but pride was at stake. As the British racing green Jaguar pulled ahead of the silver

Mercedes on a fast downhill section, Hawthorn lost control of his car, which crossed the dual carriageway and finished up against a tree, killing him instantly. For a man who had seen many friends and rivals die on the track, this seemed a strangely sad and even inglorious way to go.

A few weeks earlier Hawthorn had surprised Enzo Ferrari by telling him that he would not be defending his title in 1959. There was clearly a vacancy for a number-one driver at Maranello, and Vandervell's withdrawal from the sport had left Moss at a loose end, needing a quick solution to the problem of what to drive in Formula 1. But it was not to apply for the job that Moss wrote to Ferrari in March. The reverse, in fact.

In the letter he said that he had recently been asked by a journalist why he would not be driving for the Scuderia. 'I hope my answers were fair, but I feel that I would like you to hear them directly from me.' The first was that he felt racing benefited when the top drivers were spread between the top teams. The second related to the debacle at Bari in 1951, and his disappointment at the 'shattering' blow of being told, having made his way down to Puglia, that there was no car available for him. He finished by expressing his admiration for Signor Ferrari, for his cars and his drivers, and hoping 'that I shall be able to match your team with my little Cooper'.

Ferrari responded immediately to what he described as a 'curious' letter, his words suggesting it was simply destiny's fault that he could not include among his squad of drivers the one he had publicly nominated as the best in the world. He signed off with cordial greetings.

As Moss had suggested with his reference to 'my little Cooper', the answer to the dilemma was to resume his partnership with the man whose car he had driven to victory in Buenos Aires a year earlier.

Born in 1917, brought up in a hundred-room mansion on an estate in Wiltshire, Robert Ramsay Campbell Walker was in the habit of filling in the space in his passport requiring him to describe his occupation with the word 'gentleman'. He had seen his first Grand Prix at the age of seven, in Boulogne, and over the years he had become a familiar figure on the racing scene.

Before the war he used part of his fortune from the Johnnie Walker whisky company to buy a Delahaye, which he co-drove with his fellow Cambridge man Ian Connell at Le Mans in 1939. They finished eighth, Walker driving the last twelve hours after Connell's feet had been burned too badly by leaking exhaust gases to allow him to continue. Walker drove the whole race in a pinstriped suit and stopped before the finish to share his pit crew's last bottle of champagne.

While serving with the Fleet Air Arm during the war he promised his new wife that he would not return to driving racing cars in peacetime. But the agreement said nothing about entering them, and in 1949 he took the Delahaye back to Le Mans with two other drivers. The car also finished third in the French Grand Prix at Reims, held for sports cars that year, although the adventure was marred when one of the drivers was arrested for trying to smuggle several thousand watches back to England. The car was impounded and Walker had to pay £300 to get it back. Undeterred, he continued to enter cars in various categories for a cast of drivers including Tony Rolt, Peter Collins and Tony Brooks. Pairing up with Moss for the Argentinian Grand Prix at the beginning of 1958 took him into the top flight of racing, an increasingly professional world to which he brought a reminder of the old amateur ethos.

To some, Moss's decision seemed like madness. No one had ever won the world title driving for a private entrant. Not having a works car meant no access to the latest technical developments, to the full array of a factory's services, or to the help of teammates. Walker bought the Cooper-Climax, now fitted with a 2.5-litre engine, and had it painted in his own colours, those of Scotland – dark blue with a white stripe around the nose, which coincidentally acknowledged Moss's lineage on his mother's side. But the private entry would always be one stage of development behind the works machines. John Cooper, too, had refused to sell Walker one of his modified Citroën gearboxes, which his number one driver, Jack Brabham, had developed into a perfect and reliable fit with the Climax engine. The solution was found by Alf Francis, now installed as Walker's chief mechanic. Francis recommended that they order special gearboxes from the Modena workshop of Valerio Colotti, familiar to him from his former role as Maserati's transmission expert.

Moss had acquired a liking for the status of underdog – or at least a relish for the challenge of taking on the superior might of the factory teams, particularly Ferrari. By this stage, too, his priorities seemed to have changed – or so he argued long afterwards, in an interview with Philip Porter. 'I raced because I enjoy racing,' he said. 'At the time I was lucky enough to be good enough to make some money, so therefore it was not necessary for me to go anywhere else. Rob was a lovely man. The whole crew were a great team, and at the time we were as good as any other team, I reckon. And of course the freedom I got with Rob was important.

If I wanted to go anywhere in the world, if he half-agreed he would send the car. Also I could race any other cars I wanted to race wherever I wanted to race them. We would test and do all the things we normally did. I just found it more enjoyable.'

It could be said that Moss's reputation for having an excessive interest in money was undermined by his arrangement with Walker. In five years together, their agreement was based on nothing more than a handshake. And, as he said, the non-exclusive relationship allowed him to go off and do other things outside Formula 1, such as sharing victory in the 1959 sports car championship as the lead driver in the Aston Martin team. Midway through that season, after gearbox failures with the Cooper in the first two rounds of the world championship, Moss was even able to switch, with Walker's blessing, to a BRM run by the British Racing Partnership, a team recently formed by his manager, Ken Gregory, and his father, and in which he had an interest.

He had tried BRM's latest model, the P25, in a private session at Goodwood over the Easter weekend, posting the circuit's first 100mph lap. He agreed to drive it at the International Trophy at Silverstone, and was going well until the front brakes failed at 130mph, giving him a nasty moment. When BRM finally won a world championship grand prix, at Zandvoort in May with Jo Bonnier at the wheel, an agreement was made to borrow a car, paint it in Moss's old favourite colours – pale green with white wheels – and enter it for him in two Grands Prix in July. On a hot day at Reims the car went well, although unable to match Tony Brooks's winning Ferrari, until Moss spun on melting tar and could not restart, the clutch already having broken.

He tried pushing it back to the pits, as he had done with his Cooper in 1951, but this time the car was heavier, the distance was greater and the heat got the better of him. At Aintree, where the field was depleted by the absence of the Ferrari team, thanks to a labour dispute in Italy, he finished a slightly devalued second to Jack Brabham's Cooper after fuel-feed problems and a long pit stop.

Back in Walker's Cooper for the German Grand Prix at AVUS, he had qualified second on the high-speed track in Berlin, managing to clock 196mph on one of the long straights in the little car. The gearbox broke during the race, which was at least a gentler fate than the one awaiting BRP's BRM, which ejected its new driver, Hans Herrmann, while cartwheeling to destruction after its brakes failed at the end of one of the long straights. But the Cooper redeemed itself with wins from pole position at Lisbon – where he lapped the entire field – and Monza, representing a considerable feat for the single-car team against the more powerful Ferraris of Brooks, Phil Hill and Dan Gurney. The Colotti box had defied Moss's critics by holding up for two victories in a row.

There would be a three-month wait before the final round of the championship. At Sebring, Moss, Brooks and Brabham were all in contention for the title. Once again Stirling needed to win and take the fastest lap. Brooks was removed from contention when he was rammed in the rear by his young teammate Wolfgang von Trips on the opening lap. Keeping a promise he had made to his wife, he stopped to check that there was no significant damage, thus putting himself out of contention and incurring the wrath of the team's management for what was seen as his excessive caution. After five laps Moss held the lead, comfortably ahead of the works

Coopers of Brabham and Bruce McLaren, when the gearbox failed again, handing the title to the Australian.

Defending his driver against widespread accusations of being a car-breaker, Walker wrote in *Autosport*: 'I'm sure all those for whom he has driven will tell you that Stirling takes it out of himself, not the car. People forget the times he has won with no water, no clutch, no oil pressure.'

Still there were many who claimed that this anticlimax represented just the latest example of Moss paying dearly for what they saw as his fatal flaw: a seemingly incurable need to complicate things in the desire to find a winning edge, when all he really needed was to be in a factory team that put him on level terms with his rivals and then to let his genius make the difference. But it was too late to change now, or so it seemed.

# CHAPTER 46

# THE PRICE

The week before Ivor Bueb died at Clermont-Ferrand in 1959, he and his wife Betty had stayed at the Moss family farm in Tring with Stirling and Katie. When it came to long-distance sports car races, Moss always needed another driver to share the work in the cockpit. Since the early '50s, the regulations had required the participation of at least two drivers per car in endurance events. Occasionally his partner was someone close to his own level of performance: a Collins, a Brooks or a Gurney. More usually it was someone of lesser stature who could be relied on to keep his end up without damaging the car or losing too much time. Bueb was one of those, and a very good one.

The owner of a garage in Cheltenham, he came late to motor racing. Aged twenty-nine when he made his debut in Formula 3 in 1952, he created a good enough impression to win a seat in the Cooper works team three years later, finishing second in the British championship. He started a handful of Grands Prix between 1957 and 1959, without scoring points, although he managed a third place in the non-championship Pau GP of 1957 at the wheel of a Connaught. In sports cars, though, he distinguished himself – particularly at Le Mans, where he co-drove a factory-entered D-type Jaguar with Hawthorn to win the tragic 1955 event, which happened to be his first race in a big sports car. He repeated the win in an Ecurie Ecosse D-type two years later, sharing the drive with Ron Flockhart.

After Archie Scott-Brown, the works Lister-Jaguar driver, had died in a crash at Spa in 1958, Bueb became his replacement. In February of the following year he was teamed with Moss for the Sebring 12 Hours, in the latest three-litre Lister-Jaguar with an aerodynamic body designed by Frank Costin. Briggs Cunningham, who had entered Moss's winning OSCA in 1954, was the official entrant, and the car was painted in his team colours: white with a double blue stripe down the bonnet.

Bueb took the first stint and was holding fifth place when he handed over to Moss after two and a half hours. Steadily Moss worked his way past the works Ferrari Testa Rossas into the lead, increasing his margin when, unusually for the Florida circuit, heavy rain began to fall and turned into a prolonged cloudburst. After six hours he was still at the wheel when the car ran out of petrol on the far side of the circuit. The mechanics had missed one of the churns during the last refuelling stop. Moss jumped out and persuaded a marshal to give him a lift back to the pits on his motor scooter, hoping to grab a can of fuel and take it back to the car. To the team's astonishment, the car was disqualified on the grounds that its driver had contravened the regulations by failing to return to the pits on foot.

Four months later Moss and Bueb were both on the start line for the Trophée d'Auvergne, a Formula 2 race at the Charade circuit in the hills outside Clermont-Ferrand, a mini Nürburgring offering a challenge and a spectacle. Both men were in Coopers fitted with Borgward engines. Moss's car was entered by Rob Walker, Bueb's by Ken Gregory's British Racing Partnership, which was funding its efforts by pioneering the idea of title sponsorship of a team, in this case from a hire-purchase company called Yeoman Credit. Taking his place on pole position, Moss was forced to back off when the starter, the notoriously erratic Toto Roche, dropped his flag while standing directly in front of the Englishman, who gesticulated furiously for Roche to get out of his way. Bueb's Yeoman Credit teammate, the brilliant 21-year-old Chris Bristow, led the opening laps, but eventually Moss took over and cruised to victory.

Bueb, however, lost control during a sequence of high-speed curves and smashed into an earth bank while trying to fend off Maurice Trintignant in the second Walker Cooper. Thrown out as the car rolled, he lay motionless on the track next to his wrecked machine, his helmet torn off. Three gendarmes and a marshal took one limb each and carried him away from the circuit while the remaining competitors continued to roar past. An ambulance arrived to take him to the hospital in Clermont-Ferrand, where a ruptured spleen was diagnosed among his injuries. Bristow, to whom he had been something of a mentor, stayed on with him until he died there six days later.

Betty Bueb was looked after by Katie Moss, who remained in France while her husband went off to Berlin to prepare for the next race. The victim in Germany that weekend would be Jean Behra, Stirling's former Maserati teammate, thrown out of his Porsche over the rim of the AVUS banking and killed when his flying body hit a flagpole. When Stirling got home from Berlin, he and Katie stayed up talking until four in the morning in what may have been their only proper conversation about her inability to live with so many deaths. 'The drivers were detached,' Katie told Philip Porter. 'The wives couldn't be.'

'Fear is a lack of understanding of what is happening': John Freeman's questions on *Face to Face* in 1960 lead Moss to talk about crashes, money, God and marriage (BBC).

# CHAPTER 47

# *FACE TO FACE*

The news of the end of Moss's marriage had broken a few weeks before he was accorded an honour almost the equal of his OBE: an appearance in June 1960 as the subject of *Face to Face*, a weekly half-hour BBC television series in which famous people were interviewed by John Freeman, a pioneer in the art of interrogation on the small screen.

Moss was the seventeenth of the programme's thirty-five subjects during its three seasons, his turn coming after Bertrand Russell, Dame Edith Sitwell and Adlai Stevenson, and only three weeks after the riveting (and, to many, disturbing) edition in which the comedian Tony Hancock had been stripped bare, psychologically speaking, in front of the cameras. Freeman's most memorable success would come when he reduced the TV personality Gilbert Harding to tears by questioning him about his relationship with his mother.

For the programme's makers, the timing of the Moss interview could hardly have been better. He had also just been banned from driving on the road for a year and fined £50 after being found guilty of dangerous driving by a court in Shrewsbury, following a head-on collision. Freeman would not miss the opportunity, but he was shrewd enough to take his time.

After the title sequence, featuring charcoal sketches of the subject by the artist Feliks Topolski, he began by asking whether Moss ever thought about death while racing. 'Not when I'm driving,' came the reply. 'But I am frightened of death. It's something which I think every driver should ... or possibly it helps him to be frightened. Because if you're not frightened of an accident, then what is your limitation?'

From the start, Moss was responding in his slightly clipped voice – a reminder that, near the start of his career, he had taken elocution lessons – with swift, fluent and thoughtful answers, occasionally correcting himself or going back to amplify a point he was trying to make. 'Fear is really a lack of understanding of what is happening,' he continued. 'Like when you're a child, you're frightened of the dark because you don't understand what's there. If you come into a corner and you're going at what you consider is fast enough, and suddenly something happens, then you get frightened. Or at least after you've tried to sort out the mess you're in, then you get frightened.'

Was he conscious that death was very close if he made a mistake? 'No. Not when I'm driving. I am when I think about it, but I prefer not to. Death is something which frightens me, but thinking about it doesn't make it any less likely to happen, therefore I don't think about it.' Was it all as risky as spectators imagined? 'It's a calculated risk, but there are unfortunately things which you can't calculate for, which are mechanical failure or oil on the track.'

Did he believe in God? 'Yes, I do. I'm not religious, though.'

Did he ever have a thought of that kind, in a moment of fear, that he wanted to pray or that he was close to God? 'No. Because invariably when you have an accident, you've got so much to think about. Self-preservation comes before everything. But I must admit that if I think about it now, I trust that God is with me and helping me.

'I'm religious,' he continued, 'in that I think there's a God. I'm not religious in that I don't believe in going to church. I had too much of it thrust down my throat when I was at school. I don't feel that I'm any better going to church and standing up singing hymns or praying with a lot of other people than I am on my own.'

(Thirty years later, when asked about his religious beliefs, Ayrton Senna would say: 'If I go to church, I go on my own and I like to be there alone. I find more peace that way.')

They talked about money. Did he care about it? 'A fair amount.' Did he save it against the time when he'd have to retire? 'Yes, I do. Perhaps too much. Less than I did a year ago.' Was he a rich man? 'I suppose you'd say I'm fairly prosperous. I've got expensive tastes, yes. There are quite a lot of things I want that I haven't got. But I prefer it that way. I don't think I'd like to have everything I want. I find certain things in life frustrating, and I think that would increase the frustration. I like taking a pretty girl out. I like a luxurious flat. Funnily enough, cars don't worry me too much.'

If he were to stop racing, what might replace it? He didn't know, but it wouldn't be what people usually meant by retirement. 'I can't relax. I don't want to relax. I think my friends find it rather annoying at times. I can't just go and lie on a beach and get some sun. I have to be spear-fishing or water-skiing or something like that.'

Racing drivers were popularly thought of as people who lived it up. Did he? 'Well, this is a complete change-around. When I started racing, I was much more of a hermit. Right up until very recently I took it easy for a few days before a race. I didn't go out and so on. What good did it do me? I didn't get the world championship or anything else. So I suddenly thought, let's live it up a bit. Now this year I have been. I've been out dancing – not the night before a race, but up till a couple of nights before – I've been really swinging it and having a lot of fun and it doesn't seem to have yet affected my driving, and my personal and social life is a lot more fun.'

And then, towards the very end of the half-hour interview, Freeman arrived at the questions to which everything else seemed to have been an overture. 'How much have you been affected by the two very heavy blows you've had recently? You've lost your wife and you've lost your British driving licence, in very quick succession. Did this upset you greatly?'

Guests on *Face to Face* were never given the questions before the cameras started turning. When Aristotle Onassis demanded advance notice, he was refused and did not appear. Moss must have guessed he would be asked about these issues, and his response was instant and straightforward.

'Well, actually,' he replied, 'I had trouble in business and other things – and they were all dwarfed by the trouble I had with my wife. It did upset me very much at the time, yes. Now I try to take the view that it's no good worrying about it. My wife has a life to lead and so have I. And if I worried, it would be very bad for my racing, in other words for my life, and that's why I'm trying to push it to the back of my mind.'

Freeman: 'This leads me to ask a very candid question indeed: are you fit to be married while still in active racing?'

Moss: 'Not really. It's very difficult for the wife, it's very difficult for the husband. The last thing you want is a woman who's worrying you. My wife didn't. She was very good that way. But I think it's difficult for a woman not to, and you're conscious obviously of the fact that she should be and is, obviously, worried. Also I would like children and it's bad in racing to have children because it must slow you up a bit – I think, anyway. And if you slow up a little bit, you drop an awful long way back. And if you're a professional racing driver, you're in there to win. Otherwise you should be doing something else.'

Could he marry a woman who said she'd marry him if he gave up racing? 'Yes, I think it would be possible. But there again I must qualify it: I don't know that it would be the answer. Because to give up something that is so much of your life and means so much to you – you can't say it means as much to your wife because it's so different – but something that means so much, I don't I know if that would work. It's too difficult a problem. It's something you have to take when it comes up. I don't really think that if I'd stopped racing it would have saved my marriage.'

And, yes, the other heavy blow: did he feel he should have lost his driving licence? 'I'm satisfied in my own mind that it should not have been taken away. If my name had been John Smith, it wouldn't have been taken away.' But his name was Stirling Moss.

# CHAPTER 48

# SHUNT

'Shunt. Back. Legs. Nose. Bruises. Bugger.' That, recorded in his diary, was his summary of the accident that blighted 1960, a season that might have seen him finally fulfilling his ultimate ambition. The year had started well, with sports car wins in a Maserati in the Cuban Grand Prix and, co-driving with Dan Gurney, the Nürburgring 1,000kms. Rob Walker's Cooper-Climax, which had won two of the last three Grands Prix of the preceding season, took him to third place in the Argentinian Grand Prix and second in the Glover Trophy at Goodwood, outpaced on both occasions by Innes Ireland in Colin Chapman's Lotus 18. The Cooper was quickly abandoned when Walker persuaded Chapman to sell him one of the new machines, which had immediately raised the standards of performance for a lightweight rear-engined car.

That performance came at the cost of a certain fragility, but no such problems were evident as Moss, in his first outing in the car, drove to a superb victory at Monaco, receiving the trophy from the hands of Princess Grace after thrashing the more powerful but far less nimble front-engined Ferraris and BRMs, as well as the works Lotuses and Coopers. The Lotus 18 was, he thought, an extremely sensitive car but highly responsive to his touch: 'A real driver's car, it rewarded meticulous precision and subtle chassis adjustments.'

During the practice sessions he had accepted an invitation to try the Scarab, a front-engined car built by the young Woolworth's heir Lance Reventlow, whom he had met at one of the Nassau Speed Weeks, and who was trying to launch an American F1 team with himself as one of the drivers. When Moss went out, a best time nine seconds slower around Monaco than he had recorded in his Lotus persuaded him – and probably Reventlow, too – that the day of the grand prix car with its engine at the front was well and truly over.

A week later, for the first time since the accident at Monza in 1957, he really scared himself. This was among the dunes of Zandvoort during the Dutch GP, in the same Lotus. He was lying second, close behind Jack Brabham's Cooper, when the Australian dislodged a stone slab which Moss ran over, bursting a front tyre and sending him heading towards a wood at 120mph. 'I thought I'd had it. I thought this is my lot, I'm going straight into the woods. But I managed to regain control in time or the car came back – anyway, something happened – and it was all right. I felt frightened while it was happening but immediately after I didn't get the feeling of fear because I had something else to think about. The tyre was burst, my second place was lost, I had to get back to the pits, and so on.' Rejoining the race in tenth place, he fought back to finish fourth.

Much worse was to come a fortnight later at Spa when the left rear wheel came off the Lotus at 140mph during a practice lap, the car crunching into an earth bank at barely reduced speed. That night he was flown back to St Thomas's Hospital in London, where it was discovered that he had broken both legs and crushed three vertebrae. He was astonished when his consultant had him on his feet the next day, cutting away the head-to-toe plaster cast and getting him standing for a few seconds to keep the muscles in shape. Even more amazingly to the general public, he was racing again seven weeks later, winning a sports car race at Karlskoga in Sweden in a Lotus 19 before returning to Formula 1 a week later, having missed only the Grands Prix in France and Britain as well as the Belgian round.

Walker had bought a new Lotus 18 to replace the Spa wreck in time for the Portuguese Grand Prix. Without telling Moss, he would go to the expense of buying new drive shafts and stub axles – the bits that tended to break on Lotuses, sending the wheels flying off – after every race, as a precaution against that notorious fragility. But at Oporto, Moss spun the car in the closing stages and was disqualified for push-starting it on the pavement against the direction of the race – the very thing for which he had successfully pleaded on Mike Hawthorn's behalf at the same circuit two years earlier.

This time it had no bearing on the championship. He had missed too many races, a third of the season, although he finished it off with a good win in the US Grand Prix at Riverside in California, beating Ireland's works Lotus home by forty seconds. But Brabham was the champion for a second time.

# CHAPTER 49

# RADIO ON

Rob Walker also entered Moss for races in other categories in cars bearing his colours. In 1960 there was a dumpy little Porsche Formula 2 machine, on loan from the German company and developed from their sports cars. After Alf Francis had removed the imprecise gear-change mechanism and replaced it with one left over from Moss's old Maserati 250F, the Porsche was used to win the Aintree 200, the Austrian Grand Prix, the Cape Grand Prix and the South African Grand Prix.

There were also two almost identical Ferrari 250GT Berlinettas, the short-wheelbase model which became the forerunner of the legendary 250GTO. With the first of them, owned by the stockbroker Dick Wilkins but run by Walker, Moss won the 1960 Tourist Trophy at Goodwood in a car that was ready for normal use on the road.

His victory was so comfortable that he was able to switch on the car's radio and tune in to the BBC's live commentary. His pit signals were telling him how he was doing, but on the radio he could listen to Raymond Baxter giving updates on the other competitors. 'That was quite interesting. With the helmet I wore then, I could still hear – and it's not a noisy car, it was a very quiet car, relative to racing cars, so I could keep up with what was going on right through the race.' A telegram arrived from Modena, offering Enzo Ferrari's congratulations. A year later, driving the second Walker-run 250GT SWB, Moss held off a determined assault from Mike Parkes in a similar car entered by the official UK Ferrari dealership.

Following Aston Martin's withdrawal from sports car racing, Moss was also back in the cockpit of a Maserati. The company had produced a new design, the Tipo 60/61, with a complex frame made of a seemingly infinite number of slender alloy tubes welded together, thus earning the car its nickname: the Birdcage. Maserati could no longer afford to run an official factory team, so the new cars were designed by Giulio Alfieri to be purchased and run by private owners. They had to be competitive with the new lightweight sports cars from Cooper and Lotus, but also rugged enough for the classic endurance races.

Moss was invited to Modena to test the prototype, a two-litre Tipo 60. He liked its handling and the power from its four-cylinder engine, and took it to Rouen in July 1959 for its first race, easily beating the English cars. He also suggested that a larger engine could be fitted to compete in the world championship, then restricted to three litres. When potential US purchasers also made similar requests, the engine was stretched to 2.9 litres.

Known in that form as the Tipo 61, the works-prepared car was entrusted to a young American wheeler-dealer named Lloyd 'Lucky' Casner, who had used backing from the Goodyear tyre company to put together a team he called

Camoradi, an Italian-sounding name formed from the first two letters of each word of Casner Motor Racing Division. In post-revolutionary Havana at the start of 1960, Moss drove the white and blue car to victory in the Grand Prix of Freedom despite having to sit on a broken seat for much of the race. At Sebring, he and Dan Gurney were leading the 12 Hours by a distance when the final drive failed with a third of the race left.

They had better luck at the Nürburgring, where they won the 1,000kms – Moss for the third year in a row – and vanquished the works Ferrari team with a tremendous comeback following repairs to a broken oil pipe. Both drivers took advantage of the rain that fell throughout the race, Gurney matching Moss as they exploited their skills in the mist-shrouded Eifel mountains. Next Casner wanted Moss to drive a streamlined version of the car at Le Mans, but was unable to find the $5,000 (about £1,200) the driver was asking.

The short-wheelbase 250GT and the Tipo 61 Birdcage were two of the cars whose reputations Moss did much to create. Both became highly prized by collectors of historic machinery, and in the decades that followed it was impossible to glimpse either of them without summoning the image of his figure at the wheel, putting his mature virtuosity on display and calmly outpacing the field on the way to yet another victory.

With a wave from the cockpit of Rob Walker's Lotus 18 on the Monaco harbour front in 1961, Moss acknowledges the chequered flag at the end of one of the greatest drives of his career (AP).

# CHAPTER 50

# MASTERCLASS

Moss was thirty-one when the 1961 season began, the most experienced driver in Formula 1 and by common consent the best. He had raced and won against three generations of drivers: Fangio's, his own and now a bunch of younger men, of whom the Scottish farmer Jim Clark looked the most gifted. Four times Moss had been runner-up in the drivers' championship, and twice third. Surely his bad luck could no longer continue to deny him the title he deserved.

Standing in his way was his old nemesis, Enzo Ferrari. This was a season in which the rules changed. Out went the 2.5-litre cars of the past seven years. The new Formula 1 was for cars with unsupercharged 1.5-litre engines, the same as the old Formula 2. Ferrari had used the previous seasons to develop their smaller single-seater with a new V6 engine, whereas their British rivals, unwisely believing that the unwelcome change of regulations could be overturned, had been left behind. The new Dino 156, with a distinctive twin-nostrilled snout, would prove immediately to be the fastest car in the field by a good margin. Everyone else would be trailing in the wake of the car that quickly became known as the Sharknose. When an Italian rookie, Giancarlo Baghetti, was given one of them for the non-championship Syracuse Grand Prix, an hors d'oeuvre to the season, he outpaced the Lotuses of Moss and Clark, the Porsches of Dan Gurney and Jo Bonnier, the Coopers of Jack Brabham and Bruce McLaren, and the BRMs of Tony Brooks and Graham Hill. Then Baghetti did it again in Naples, against a less formidable field. The Sharknose had sent out a warning.

But the first race of the world championship season was at Monaco, where Moss was the master. He called it 'a real drivers' circuit, where skill can make up for technical deficiencies'. In his underpowered four-cylinder Lotus-Climax he started from pole position and produced a masterclass, taking the lead on the fourteenth lap and using everything he had to stay ahead of the pursuing red cars of Richie Ginther, Phil Hill and Wolfgang von Trips, all unable to profit from the extra thirty horsepower of their engines on the tight 1.9-mile circuit, where Moss's precision and concentration paid dividends. He had removed the side panels from the car to provide extra ventilation on a baking afternoon, thus incidentally allowing spectators a clearer sight of him in action.

Later he would consider it to be the greatest victory of his career. He had driven, he thought, ninety of those 100 laps flat out – 'at ten-tenths', as he would say. It was the equivalent of asking a track athlete to run a mile at the speed of a sprinter. He had expected the Ferraris, with their superior power, to come breezing past him in the closing stages. They attacked him in relays, but somehow he stayed out of reach, finishing three and a half seconds ahead of an exhausted Ginther.

This two-hour demonstration of genius would be repeated three months later, in the German Grand Prix. In the meantime, the Ferraris had made the most of their power advantage to sweep the board at Zandvoort, Spa, Reims and Aintree, but at the fourteen-mile Nürburgring, with its 174 corners and 1,000 feet of elevation change, Moss's brilliance and racecraft would once again come into their own. In a day of changeable weather in the Eifel mountains, he decided to use Dunlop's new rain tyres; this was against the advice of the company's own technicians, who told him they would not last in the mixed conditions. He opted to take the chance, and once Jack Brabham – his Cooper fitted with the new powerful V8 Coventry Climax engine – had left the road early in the first lap, Moss led the rest of the race, increasingly heavy rain in the closing stages helping him to preserve the tyres and fend off the Ferraris of von Trips and Hill.

There was also an element of psychology involved: his reputation for brilliance in bad weather made his rivals reluctant to try to match his speed on a wet track. 'I didn't like the wet,' he told the author Peter Manso. 'Everybody thought that I did. I wasn't going to broadcast it.' He might not have liked it, but he was certainly its master. The heaviest traffic he saw all day at the Nürburgring, he said later, was on the autobahn heading for the airport at Düsseldorf that night.

In his whole career, he once remarked, he had never achieved a perfect lap. But the joy, as he explained to Ken Purdy during their collaboration on the book *All But My Life*, came in trying. 'You go through a corner absolutely flat out. Right on the ragged edge, but absolutely in control, on your own line to an inch, the car just hanging there, the tyres as good as geared to the road, locked to it, and yet you know

that if you ask one more mile an hour of the car, if you put
another five pounds of side thrust on it, you'll lose the whole
flaming vehicle as surely as if someone had smeared the road
with six inches of grease; so you stay just this side of that fraction of extra speed, that fraction of extra weight that could
ruin everything, and perhaps kill you to boot, you're on top
of it all, and the exhilaration, the thrill is tremendous, you
say to yourself, all right, you bastards, top that one, match
it, even, and you feel like a painter who has just put the last
brush-stroke on a canvas after years of trying to catch a certain expression – it's rewarding. And you must grant that it's
not monotonous. No art can be monotonous.'

He believed that driving fast was an art form, in its way,
with similarities to ballet in the emphasis on discipline,
rhythm and movement. 'Certainly it's not creative in the way
that choreography is creative or that composition of music for
ballet is creative, but I think that in execution it is comparable.' And in those two performances in 1961, at Monaco and
the Nürburgring, he raised the art to its highest level.

# CHAPTER 51

# INDUSTRIAL ACTION

He was not a natural trade unionist, but at Erlen in Switzerland in 1951 he had led a delegation of English, French and Italian drivers to complain to the organisers about the tactics of Toni Ulmen, an erstwhile German Formula 2 champion, who was exploiting the rule about overtaking only on the left by placing his outdated Veritas in the middle of the track and blocking faster cars, including Moss's HWM.

Six years later he became a member of the new Union des Pilotes Professionels Internationaux, an organisation including all the grand prix drivers of the day. Following the terrible crashes at Le Mans in 1955 and the Mille Miglia in 1957, which had taken the lives of spectators as well as competitors and brought widespread condemnation of the sport as a whole, the drivers banded together with the intention of campaigning for better safety precautions. When they boycotted the 1957 Race of Two Worlds on the Monza banking, claiming that it was too dangerous, they were accused of adopting strike tactics better suited to miners or dockworkers. After the American cars and drivers had turned up and put on a spectacular race in which no one was injured, the Europeans looked foolish. And that was more or less the end of the UPPI.

But when Fangio accepted a present from his fellow drivers to mark his retirement in 1958, his speech at the formal dinner in the Hotel Principe di Savoia in Milan included the remark that the Italian Grand Prix, held earlier that day, had been a good race because nobody had been killed. The number of fatal accidents in Formula 1 was continuing to increase, prompting the UPPI's rebirth four years later in the form of the Grand Prix Drivers' Association, which came into being in May 1961. Following an election during the week of the Monaco Grand Prix, Moss was named the body's first chairman. Its original members were listed on its headed notepaper: Stirling Moss (chairman), Joakim Bonnier (vice-chairman), Cliff Allison, Jack Brabham, Tony Brooks, Jimmy Clark, Olivier Gendebien, Richie Ginther, Masten Gregory, Dan Gurney, Graham Hill, Phil Hill, Innes Ireland, Bruce McLaren, Roy Salvadori, John Surtees, Henry Taylor, Maurice Trintignant and Wolfgang von Trips.

With only three exceptions – Hans Herrmann, Michael May and Lucien Bianchi, who were not regulars in the series – that list represented the full roll call of drivers entered for the 1961 Monaco race. What is striking is that of the nineteen founder members of the GPDA, no fewer than fifteen had English as their native language: nine were British, four were American, one was Australian and one a New Zealander. Five or six years earlier, before the great cull that removed the likes of Ascari, Marimón, de Portago, Castellotti, Musso, Behra and Schell, the proportions would have been very different, but the shift also told the story of the changing balance of power within the sport, from Italy, Germany and France to Britain. Grand Prix racing was following the lead of the diplomatic world: its working language was now English.

Moss retained the chairmanship for two years, until the formal retirement that followed his accident at Goodwood. He was succeeded first by Jo Bonnier, who served from 1963 to 1971, and then by Jackie Stewart, whose seven-year term encompassed the time in which the safety of the drivers became a much greater priority.

There had been scepticism when the GPDA was first formed, some traditionalists believing that such bodies had no place in motor sport. Those same sceptics had derided and perhaps helped smother the UPPI. Now things were different. Stewart, in particular, was appalled by the death rate in the '60s and early '70s; he and his wife had mourned the loss of so many friends that he vowed to use the organisation to pressure the governing body into accepting new ideas on safety, from the mandatory use of seat belts, flameproof clothing and certificated helmets to safer fuel tanks and the use of Armco barriers. Circuits considered hazardous were removed from the calendar. This meant the end of such landmarks as the original eight-mile Spa-Francorchamps track, the Nürburgring's majestic Nordschliefe, the wheatfields of Reims-Gueux and the vertiginous Monza banking.

Like Stewart, Moss had taken part in races and meetings in which drivers had died; nevertheless he deplored many of the changes being made in the name of safety, believing that a willingness to risk life and limb was intrinsic to the sport. 'I think part of the attraction of motor racing was the danger,' he once said to me. 'That was part of the reason you wanted to do it.' He gave Ken Purdy his opinion on featureless artificial circuits: 'To go flat out through a bend that is surrounded by level lawn is one thing, but to go flat out through a bend that has a stone wall on one side and a precipice on the other – that's an achievement.'

Tony Brooks, the least macho and most thoughtful of racing drivers, drew another parallel. 'It's the sociological factor. You're not supposed to risk your life these days. It's more than fifty years, thank goodness, since we've been involved in what you might call a proper war, so people no longer understand that life can involve a high degree of risk. Think about what happened in London during the Blitz. There were bombs raining down constantly, every day you could be killed, and people took it in their stride. "It could happen," they thought, "but it probably won't." Now people think it's abhorrent to do anything that involves risk.'

Brooks and Moss shared a love of circuits that presented the greatest challenges, but not everyone agreed. Brabham hated a place like Pescara, with its natural hazards. So did Hawthorn, who once said of the Targa Florio: 'I can raise no enthusiasm for rushing up and down mountains with hairpins all over the place and sheer drops on one side.'

In an interview in 2009, Moss compared motor racing without danger to cooking without salt: 'It's still a lovely meal, but, my god, salt would have jazzed it up a bit more.' He added that he was scared of dying. 'I didn't want to die. I had no death wish. I thought I would drive as fast as I feel safe and that would be my limit, and I stuck with that all the time.'

Another of his remarks seemed to sum up his philosophy: 'One of the reasons one races is because one wants to frighten oneself. If you go round and you're fully safe, what exhilaration are you getting?'

# CHAPTER 52

# FOUR BY FOUR

Curiosity was always a salient feature of Moss's character, particularly when it came to technical innovation. 'He was always looking for a technical advantage,' Ken Gregory said, 'even though he didn't need it.' In his quest for machinery that would give him a winning edge, sometimes his eagerness tripped him up. Occasionally, as with Ferguson's Project 99, it pointed him towards the future.

At the beginning of the '60s, road cars were driven either by the wheels at the back or, in a few slightly eccentric exceptions, such as the Citroën 2CV, the Saab 96 and BMC's Mini, at the front. Four-wheel drive was practically unheard of for anything other than utility vehicles like tractors and Land Rovers. The Ferguson-Climax P99 was the novelty of the 1961 season, a front-engined Formula 1 single-seater with an engine driving all four wheels.

Conceived by Tony Rolt, Moss's former teammate in the Jaguar sports car team, it was commissioned by Harry Ferguson, whose company was better known for manufacturing farm tractors but who wanted to demonstrate the application of four-wheel drive to other types of vehicle. When the project began, Formula 1 cars had 2.5-litre engines located in front of the driver. By the time it made it to a racetrack, all that had changed. But, unlike Aston Martin's DBR4 and Lance Reventlow's Scarab, it was not rendered immediately obsolete by the wholesale switch to a rear-engined philosophy and new regulations requiring 1.5-litre engines.

The all-wheel drive meant that the car's balance was sound even with the engine in its outdated location, and its weight was not greatly different from that of a Cooper or a Lotus. Naturally it required a very different driving technique, calling on Moss's unmatched powers of adaptability. He found it fascinating, particularly appreciating the pronounced advantage it gave in wet conditions.

Entrusted to Rob Walker (for whom Rolt had raced a Connaught) and painted in his colours, it was driven by Jack Fairman at Silverstone in the British Empire Trophy in its original 2.5-litre form and in the British Grand Prix at Aintree with a 1.5-litre engine, failing to finish in one and being disqualified for receiving a push-start in the other. Moss briefly took over from Fairman at Aintree after his own Lotus had retired, giving him the rare distinction of driving two makes of car in a single world championship race and the unique one of driving front- and rear-engined and two- and four-wheel-drive cars in the same Grand Prix.

In September he was again at the wheel of the Ferguson for the International Gold Cup at Oulton Park. Conditions were wet at the Cheshire track, suiting the car's characteristics perfectly and enabling Moss, after a poor start, to come through a field including the Coopers of Brabham and McLaren, the

BRMs of Brooks and Graham Hill, and Clark's Lotus. By the time he took his lap of honour, the rain had stopped and the parkland circuit was bathed in autumn sunshine. He had just become the only driver in history to win a Formula 1 race in a car with four-wheel drive.

Harry Ferguson had died a few months before that victory and the project lacked the backing needed to turn it into a serious proposition in Grand Prix racing. The P99 was taken to New Zealand at the end of 1962 for Graham Hill to drive in the Tasman series, and in 1963 it was sent for tests at Indianapolis, where it inspired a succession of 4WD challengers for the 500 Miles races. In 1964 Peter Westbury used it to win the British hill-climb championship, and the principles of its patented transmission came into widespread use in 4x4 vehicles from major manufacturers. Twenty years on from that Oulton Park win, with BRM, Lotus, Matra, McLaren and Cosworth all having toyed with Ferguson's innovation, four-wheel-drive was banned completely from Formula 1.

Moss retained a memory of the car as one of his favourites among the 108 he raced during his career. Its traction, he said, was so good that he could overtake even his quickest rivals around corners – on the outside. And Harry Ferguson's four-wheel-drive patent turned out be a world-beater. From west London to West Hollywood, all those supersized SUVs clogging the streets – the Range Rovers, the Q5s, the Cayennes, the X5s, the Bentaygas and the Levantes – carry a little bit of the P99's DNA.

# CHAPTER 53

# LUNCH AT THE CAVALLINO

In the autumn of 1961, between the Modena Grand Prix and the Italian GP, Moss was invited to test the prototype Ferrari 250GTO, so new that its alloy bodywork was unpainted, at Monza. He liked it very much. It was clearly a successful evolution of the old 250GT in which he had enjoyed success. In early April 1962 he and Rob Walker had lunch with Enzo Ferrari in Maranello, in the old man's private room at the Cavallino restaurant opposite the factory gates, where they discussed the possibility of a collaboration.

Ferrari received the two visitors from England in his office, a few yards from the entrance to the factory on the Via Abetone. It was through those gates that he had driven the first car to bear his name for a test run in March 1947, a couple of weeks after the teenaged Moss had made his competition debut in his father's BMW. French would have been their common language. As well as taking them across the road for lunch, where he would have shown them the genial side to the 'terrifying old man' he said had been invented by journalists, Ferrari showed them around the factory where the road cars were built alongside the racing department, then gearing up for a new season.

In his memoirs, Ferrari would bracket Moss alongside Tazio Nuvolari as men 'who, on any kind of machine, in any circumstances and over any course, risked everything to win and, in the ultimate analysis, appear to stand out amongst the rest. They knew how to give of their best whether at the wheel of a saloon car, a sports two-seater or a single-seater racing car.'

Now he was impressed by the Englishman's interest in and technical understanding of what he was being shown as he stopped to watch workmen casting aluminium cylinder heads and welding chassis tubes. 'He asked if he could look over the workshops, and showed himself astonishingly expert in the numerous things he asked about. We had a long and friendly talk. The conclusion was rather unexpected.'

Ferrari's offer was surprising. He would build a Grand Prix car according to Moss's requirements, he said – it would, of course, be an evolution of the Dino 156 which had just won the 1961 drivers' and constructors' championship – and place it at his disposal. It could be run by the Walker team and painted in the dark blue and white colours, as would a GTO to be entered in the major sports car races.

A works-supported privately entered Ferrari was not something entirely new in Formula 1. Ferrari had lent cars to the Equipe Nationale Belge, painted Belgian yellow for the drivers Paul Frère and Olivier Gendebien. He had lent one to a team called FISA, organised by a group of Italian enthusiasts promoting the country's young drivers, with spectacular results when Giancarlo Baghetti became the first man to win his debut Grand Prix at Reims in 1961. But it was still an unusual arrangement, and a unique one in the sense that here was Enzo Ferrari lending a car to a driver better than any in his own team – even though Phil Hill, the new world champion, was staying on.

'It was the car to have,' Moss told *Autosport*'s Maurice Hamilton many years later. 'Apart from anything else, I couldn't think of anyone who'd been killed in a Ferrari because of a mechanical failure. Not one. And that was saying something in those days. I'd been driving Lotus cars and there was a ten-to-one chance that something was going to fall off.' The plan was for the combination to make its debut in the non-championship *Daily Express* International Trophy at Silverstone in May, followed by a full grand prix season. Given Ferrari's dominance in 1961, during which the Scuderia's cars and drivers had won six of the season's nine grands prix and both titles, surely this was Moss's opportunity to set the seal on his career.

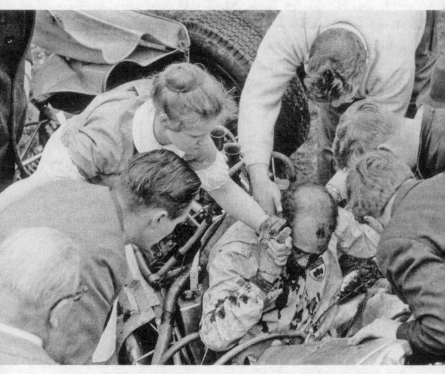

At Goodwood on Easter Monday 1962, track marshals and medical personnel gather around the crushed Lotus in the aftermath of the accident that will end Moss's career as a professional racing driver (Getty Images).

# CHAPTER 54

# EASTER MONDAY

Any court reporter knows that there are as many sides to a story as there are witnesses. That is as true of a humdrum road traffic accident as it is of a president's assassination. Or of the crash that ends a hero's career. Stirling Moss's accident at Goodwood on 23 April 1962 has its own Zapruder film, the frames from an amateur's movie camera showing the car with the number seven on its nose and flanks coming out of Fordwater, a fast right-handed curve at the back of the circuit, at about 140mph. Far away from the spectator enclosures, its driver is preparing to shape for St Mary's, the left-hander named after the parish church in the nearby hamlet of East Lavant. He is halfway round his thirty-sixth lap, with six and a half to go.

The driver's white helmet is at its usual distinctive angle. But then something unexpected happens. Instead of following the line of the track, the car heads straight onto the grass, bucking violently as its front wheels hit a hidden gully, losing speed but still travelling at about 70mph when it smashes virtually head-on into the earth bank. Soil and grass and pieces of bodywork are hurled into the air.

Among the first to arrive on the scene is a 24-year-old photographer. Michael Cooper is a regular at the Steering Wheel Club and acquainted with most of the top British drivers, who sometimes buy prints of his work. Unusually, he has been taking photographs from this rather remote part of the circuit rather than the more obvious locations. Within seconds of the accident, he runs across the track towards the wrecked car. He thinks he sees Moss momentarily trying to lift himself out of the cockpit before his head falls sideways.

When track marshals arrive, they find the car has crumpled at the front, the radiator and suspension smashed back towards the cockpit, where the unconscious driver is slumped over the twisted steering wheel. The tubes of the car's frame are bent around him. As the race goes on, a St John ambulance arrives with the medical crew. Alfred Moss is there quickly; his wife remains in the pits. Moss's helmet is removed, revealing the effects of a blow to the left side of his face. There is blood on his overalls.

A 19-year-old nurse, Annie Strudwick, from St Richard's Hospital in Chichester, is there as a volunteer; she sees his face turning purple, guesses that he has swallowed a piece of chewing gum and reaches into his mouth to hook it out. Now she holds his gloved right hand as the chassis tubes are cut and bent. (They will stay in touch: 'You were there when I needed you most,' he writes when dedicating a copy of his autobiography to her years later.) Miraculously, although petrol is pouring from ruptured pipes, there is no fire throughout the forty-five minutes it takes to free him and lift the unconscious body onto a stretcher. By that time the race is long over.

The car is Rob Walker's hybrid Lotus 18/21, now with sleeker bodywork and a V8 Climax engine. For this race, the Glover Trophy for Formula 1 cars, it has been passed on to the British Racing Partnership and a pit crew run by Tony Robinson and painted pale green. Stirling has raced it twice already in the recent weeks, in the Brussels GP and the Lombank Trophy at Snetterton. This morning, while leaving his hotel in Chichester, he has reversed his Lotus Elite into a concrete post. In the race, he gets a poor start. He has been lying third in the opening stages, behind Graham Hill's BRM and Bruce McLaren's Cooper, before John Surtees goes past in his new Lola, pushing him down to fourth. There are problems with the Lotus's gear linkage. He stops at the pits to get it fixed and sets off again, now a lap down on the leader. He matches Surtees' fastest lap, but he is still in seventh place as he comes out of Fordwater, closing on Hill, the leader, and preparing to unlap himself.

After the accident he is taken first to the hospital in Chichester and then transferred to the Atkinson Morley Hospital in Wimbledon, where he is attended by a consultant neurosurgeon, Wylie McKissock. He is in a coma and will not regain full consciousness for thirty-eight days. He is paralysed down his left side for six months. His left cheekbone is crushed, the eye socket displaced. His left leg is broken at the knee and ankle, with deep cuts. His left arm is broken, as is his nose. Much worse than any of that, the heavy impact of his head with the steering wheel has jarred his brain so badly that its right side has detached itself. When he finally awakes, his only memory of that day will be of denting his road car while leaving the hotel that morning. The blank spaces will never be filled, the dots never joined.

The crash made the lead item in the *Daily Telegraph*. The newspapers vied with each other to provide an explanation, commissioning maps and diagrams to show where and how the Lotus had left the track. A careful examination of the wrecked car by Tony Robinson showed that nothing appeared to have broken before it left the road. One suggestion, from a distant eyewitness, was that Hill had been shown a blue flag at Fordwater to warn him of Moss's approach and had lifted his left hand in acknowledgement, giving Moss the false impression that he could overtake to the left of the BRM, only to find Hill holding the normal racing line, forcing him to avoid a collision by taking to the grass at full speed.

Hill had seen the pale green Lotus going off and hitting the bank. The next time round, he slowed to a stop. He saw Michael Cooper and asked, 'Is he all right?' Then he restarted and went on to win the race. Later he spoke to Aileen Moss, who remembered him saying something like, 'I'm sorry – I didn't mean to do it.' But there was no definitive explanation of the accident – and, of course, Moss himself was left with no memory of it.

While he was recovering, Gregory attempted to short-circuit the intense press interest in the condition of the national hero by contacting Basil Cardew of the *Daily Express*, asking the enormous sum of £10,000 for an interview and a photo session. To his surprise, the newspaper's management agreed to the deal. Moss was barely coherent in his conversation with Cardew, but the interview glossed over the reality of his recovery and served the short-term purpose of satisfying the public's curiosity.

Three weeks after the accident, Enzo Ferrari unexpectedly sent a car to Silverstone for Innes Ireland to drive in the International Trophy. It was painted red, with a pale green BRP stripe down the bonnet. Ferrari had kept his promise, but in the changed circumstances no one really knew why he had made this somewhat enigmatic gesture. It was a 1961 car, and Ireland finished an unspectacular fourth.

Had the crash never happened, how would the partnership of Moss and Ferrari have worked out? Unexpectedly, 1962 turned out to be as dismal for the Scuderia as 1961 had been triumphant. The British teams, particularly BRM, Lotus and Cooper, benefited from new engines matching the power of the Italian cars, and their chassis were superior. A bout of internal warfare at Ferrari, including rows between senior personnel and Enzo's abrasive wife, Laura, resulted in the sudden defection of many of the top engineers, including Carlo Chiti, the designer of the Sharknose. Richie Ginther, the team's most experienced test and development driver, had left for a better deal at BRM.

Eight months later, with the world championship season over, one second place and two thirds for Phil Hill, the defending world champion, a third for Lorenzo Bandini and two fourth places for Ricardo Rodriguez and Giancarlo Baghetti were all the works drivers could manage as the Scuderia Ferrari plunged to fifth place in the constructors' table, behind four British teams. Given the scale of that debacle, perhaps by mid-season a disillusioned Moss would have been back in one of Walker's Lotuses, once more fighting against the odds. On the other hand, he might have stuck it out through two difficult seasons and, in 1964, taken the title that would go to John Surtees in one of the cars from Maranello.

As it was, his return to something approaching normal life took months. Finally, he went home from the hospital, with eyes that were now slightly misaligned after the surgery to rebuild the left socket. In July he flew off for a holiday in Nassau, trying to recover his strength. All the time he was being asked when he would be back in the cockpit. 'I'll race in four weeks!' had been a headline when he was discharged. Soon he realised that the truth was very different. But almost exactly a year after the accident he persuaded himself to return to a deserted Goodwood and take the wheel of BRP's Lotus 19 sports car, which he had last raced at Nassau eighteen months earlier, to see for himself whether his powers were now so reduced that he would have to retire or whether he still had a future as the world's greatest racing driver.

He circulated for a while, testing his reactions. Although the track was damp after morning rain, his lap times were respectable. But something was missing. For a racing driver, an empty track offers the opportunity to establish a flow, a rhythm, in which everything comes naturally. That wasn't happening. Things that had felt natural and intuitive for so long now appeared to require conscious calculation. After half an hour, or about twenty laps, he returned to the pits and switched the engine off. When he got out of the car, he had already decided that it was all over. In his mind he was preparing a statement that would be issued to the world within hours. The date was 1 May 1963.

Some suggested that having taken an insurance payout – it was £8,000 – he didn't feel like giving it back. A more likely reason is that he didn't want to risk returning to the top flight as a lesser version of the Stirling Moss everyone remembered. Once, talking about comebacks, he mentioned Fangio and said: 'I wouldn't have liked him to come back and not be himself.'

Reflecting on the decision years later, he thought he might have been wiser to wait a little longer. Before the accident, he had intended to continue racing at the top level all the way through his thirties and even beyond. Had he left it another year, perhaps two, his senses might have knitted themselves together into the old neural network of perception and response. He might have been able to charge down the hill to the Mirabeau corner in a Formula 1 car once again and change gear and steer while waving to a pretty girl watching from a café terrace, doing everything at racing speed. Maybe he had cheated himself of that chance.

# CHAPTER 55

# A TOY STORY

Towards the end of the race in Pescara in 1957, the half-dozen cars still running passed by at such infrequent intervals that parents who had come out of their houses to watch the Grand Prix were allowing their children to play on the road – the racetrack! – knowing that the sound of a high-revving racing engine would give them plenty of warning to get out of the way. The Vanwall, however, approached in something close to silence, its exhaust note nearer to the purr of a Rolls-Royce than the yelp of a Ferrari. And two decades after its heyday, the sound of the four-cylinder engine still gave little indication of the power lying beneath its graceful bonnet.

Too young to see a Vanwall in real action, I'd spent many childhood hours lying on a bedroom carpet, pushing a Dinky Toy version of the car, with its white-helmeted driver, around imaginary Monacos and Monzas, a ghostly crowd cheering on the British hero. For the Italian Grand Prix of 1979, twenty-two years after his win at Monza with Tony Vandervell's team, Stirling Moss had been invited to take part in a parade of old Formula 1 cars. They would assemble in the square in front of the Duomo in Milan before making their way to the circuit on roads closed for the duration of the cavalcade, a very Italian spectacle.

Moss would be driving a Vanwall, while Fangio would take part in an Alfa Romeo 159, the car with which he had won his first world championship in 1951. There was also a little Gordini to be driven by Maurice Trintignant, once a double winner of the Monaco Grand Prix and subsequently the mayor of Vergèze, a village in southern France. Trintignant's nickname was Le Petoulet – a reference to the rat droppings which had clogged the carburettor of his Bugatti when it emerged from wartime storage for Coupe de la Libération in 1945. When he began producing wine from his vineyard in Vergèze, Le Petoulet was the name emblazoned on the label of his bottles. Now sixty-two years old, he smiled at a group of us standing nearby in the Piazza del Duomo, admiring the neat blue car, and invited us to give him a push-start: the realisation of a small boy's dream.

The next day I was sitting with a friend in a grandstand between the two Lesmo corners, awaiting the start of the race in which Jody Scheckter could secure the points that would make him Ferrari's seventh world champion. And so it came to pass, with Gilles Villeneuve in the second Ferrari sitting diligently on the South African's tail, almost certainly the faster of the two but loyally aware that, on this occasion, the priority was a title for the team's number one. Villeneuve's unselfishness evoked the gestures of earlier days. He was not yet thirty years old and his time, he felt sure, would come.

Sadly, Villeneuve would not live to reap the reward for his gesture. He and Scheckter stayed with the team for the following season, but the Ferrari of 1980 proved no match for its English rivals, whose understanding of the new science of ground effects left the Scuderia floundering and the South African unable to mount a defence of his title.

When Scheckter retired at the end of that season, Villeneuve was naturally seen as the heir apparent, but a season of struggle with Ferrari's first turbocharged car yielded only wins in Monaco and Spain.

The following year held out greater promise, but after a bitter and unresolved dispute over team orders with Pironi at Imola, where they finished first and second, he was killed in practice at Zolder, aged thirty-two. There would be no world title, but many had admired the way he put a championship second to the simpler desire to win every race he started. The chequered flag, not the accumulation of points, was the vision that motivated him.

He had established a special place in the affections of Enzo Ferrari, who saw in his displays of high-wire daring and inexhaustible competitive spirit some of the qualities he associated with Nuvolari and Moss, and for which he could forgive the occasional indiscretion. 'His generosity, his enthusiasm, not to mention the way he broke stub-axles, gearboxes, clutches, and brakes on his way to the finish line, taught us a great deal about how to defend a driver when some sudden need arose,' the Old Man would write. For the little French-Canadian's exhibition of unselfish loyalty on this day at Monza, Ferrari was probably as grateful as he had been twenty-three years earlier, when Peter Collins gave up his car at the same circuit so that Fangio could win his fourth title.

An hour before the start of the Grand Prix, we were cheering the other sight for which we'd come. First Fangio blasted past in the supercharged Alfetta, a sight from the black-and-white images of the immediate post-war years now visible in full colour: the deep red of the bodywork vivid against the green of the foliage in the Monza park and the sombre grey of the track. Soon, heralded by that low murmur, came the dark green car, its cockpit occupied by the man in the white Herbert Johnson helmet. The Vanwall was never a dramatic sight, but its smooth aerodynamic shape, as profound a tribute to the 1950s idea of stylish design as a Hawker Hunter or a Parker 51, possessed a kind of dignity befitting its age, even as Moss guided it at what seemed close to racing speed through the two right-handers and off down towards what was once known, before the introduction of chicanes, as the Curva Vialone. The Dinky Toy had come to life.

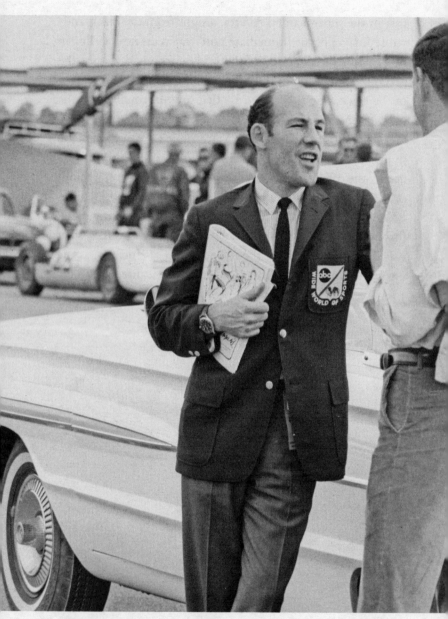

Now a former racing driver, Moss pursues a new career as a commentator for ABC's *Wide World of Sports* at the Daytona International Speedway in 1964 (Stanley Rosenthal/ Revs Institute).

# CHAPTER 56

# BEING STIRLING

'It would be very difficult to give up motor racing,' he'd told John Freeman during their *Face to Face* interview in 1960. 'I don't know quite what would be a substitute for the exhilaration, the excitement, the travel and all the other things. I'm not really qualified for any particular business, so it's going to be hard to give it up.'

What he did was construct a life that allowed him to carry on being the Stirling Moss everyone remembered, earning a living from their residual affection and respect. It took a while to adjust to that new life, and the transition was difficult. To hide the scars on his face while they healed, he grew a beard. He and Ken Gregory parted company after ten years of a close and successful relationship. Strains became apparent when Moss, struggling to recover from his injuries, began to question the way BRP and Stirling Moss Ltd were being run.

Ivor Bueb, Chris Bristow and Harry Schell had been killed in BRP's Coopers: each one through driver error or bad luck. BRP tried building their own cars, first for

Formula 1 and then for Indianapolis, but with little success. Moss and Gregory finally severed their business partnership in 1965. Later Gregory went into the air taxi business, but his career would always be defined by one relationship. His biography, on which he collaborated with the writer Robert Edwards, was called *Managing a Legend*. His former client, a man now denied his accustomed means of self-expression, would not be easy for anyone to live with for a while, no matter how much freedom he had been given to pursue his other interests.

He had been retired from racing for four or five years when I was sent, as a cub reporter for a local evening newspaper in the English Midlands, to report on the opening of a new car dealership, normally the most uninspiring of assignments. But the promise of an appearance by Stirling Moss lifted it out of the regular reporting schedule of funerals, golden weddings, juvenile court hearings, road traffic accidents and the occasional factory fire. He was there when I arrived, and so was a pre-war Bugatti in which he was giving joyrides. I settled into the passenger seat and we set off for a spin up and down a dual carriageway. It was almost as much of a thrill as if I'd been riding alongside him in his Mille Miglia victory in 1955, as the journalist Denis Jenkinson so famously did.

Giving others a vicarious taste of what that might have been like became part of his job, in all sorts of settings and circumstances. Thirty years after the jaunt in the Bugatti, by which time I was working for a national newspaper, he gave me a ride down the hill at Goodwood during a press day for the annual Festival of Speed. Sitting behind him in a beautifully finished silver-bodied two-seater soapbox cart, powered only by gravity but steered by a master, feeling like a

10-year-old again, I told him: 'You be Moss and I'll be Jenks.' The man in the white helmet had the grace to chuckle.

His links with the sport were maintained when he joined ABC's *Wide World of Sports*, commentating on Formula 1 and the NASCAR series for the American television audience between 1962 and 1980. From 1963 to 1966 he ran his own team, called SMART (Stirling Moss Automobile Racing Team), entering Sir John Whitmore, Innes Ireland and other drivers in cars including a Lotus Elan, a Porsche 904 and a Lola sports car; a BRP was driven in non-championship F1 races by Richie Ginther.

Eventually, without a great deal of fuss, he returned to racing. He was to be seen in historic events in the 1970s, sometimes – in an example of cognitive dissonance for those to whom Moss in a red single-seater meant a Maserati – at the wheel of a Ferrari Dino 246 replica, an exact recreation of the last front-engined car to win a world championship Grand Prix. He also tried a return to contemporary racing in Audi's team of saloon cars, but faced the discovery that the old driving techniques were no longer applicable to modern cars with wide slick tyres, and that etiquette among racing drivers had taken a turn for the worse.

He wasn't used, he said, to motor racing being a contact sport, as it had become for those who had grown up racing karts. In his era, the likes of the cold-blooded Nino Farina and the hot-headed Willy Mairesse were the rare exceptions to the rule of drivers racing hard but knowing they held each other's lives in their hands. In his two years in the British Saloon Car Championship, the only time he enjoyed the Audi was when it rained and the slick tyres were replaced with treaded rubber, enabling his special touch to show itself once again.

Later still he acquired a series of his own historic cars to drive at suitable meetings, choosing from a gene pool of pretty sports-racing cars from around 1960 with small-capacity engines and good handling. There were cars he'd never raced in anger, like the Wiki, built by a Belgian enthusiast, and a lovely Lola Mk 1. And those which evoked great moments from his personal history, including an OSCA, which reminded him of the car he'd used to win at Sebring in 1954, and a Porsche RS60 like the one with which he and Graham Hill had almost won the 1961 Targa Florio. These were cars in which he could display an artistry easily appreciated from the grandstands.

Max Mosley, president of the FIA, the international governing body, waived the usual strict regulations on safety equipment by giving him permission to wear his original helmet and overalls in historic races, and to compete in cars without seat belts or other safety devices, making him the only man ever to receive such a dispensation. Thus were the crowds who flocked to see him in historic car events around the world allowed a glimpse of how he looked in his prime, as well as the chance to appreciate the sight of a perfectly controlled four-wheel drift.

In later years he was a valued guest at events from the Concours d'Elégance at Palm Beach in Florida to the Festival of Speed at Goodwood. He gave his name to a special edition of Mercedes' SLR McLaren supercar, liveried to resemble his Mille Miglia winner, and to a recreation of the green and yellow Lister-Jaguar in which he had won the supporting race to the 1958 British Grand Prix.

He had been attracting queues of autograph hunters since very early in his career, and he was invariably patient, courteous and obliging. But eventually, realising that he was being asked to sign photographs and books simply so that they could be put up for immediate resale, he insisted on adding an individual dedication.

The magnetism of his presence seemed only to increase. Somehow the fact that his attendance at an event had been bought and paid for never diminished the thrill felt by even the most jaded enthusiast from proximity to a man in whom so much history reposed. Only one other retired racing driver brought more charisma to a public gathering: Juan Manuel Fangio, his friend for life. And when Fangio died in 1995, aged eighty-four, Moss travelled to Balcarce to be one of the six pallbearers at the parish church of San José, the crowd outside estimated at 10,000.

He never stopped working. From early in his adult life he had followed his father's advice to invest in bricks and mortar, and not just for his own use. Gradually he built up a small property empire, buying residential buildings and letting them to tenants. By 2010 he had forty-five tenants in ten London properties, divided into flats or bedsits, spread across West Kensington, Maida Vale, Pimlico and Battersea – all within a ten-minute ride of his office. 'I always stay within scooter distance of my office so if someone calls to say the washing machine is broken, I can get on my bike and go over myself to try and fix it.' He had never borrowed funds to expand his property empire. 'It may sound like a good idea on paper, but borrowing against one property to buy another seems to me like building up a house of cards – it will only come crashing down later.'

In March 2010, aged eighty, he was talking to someone while waiting for the lift to arrive on the second floor of his high-tech home in Shepherd Street. When the doors opened, he stepped in. But there was no cabin. It was stuck on the floor above. He fell 30 feet down the empty shaft onto the concrete base, breaking both ankles and several bones in his feet and chipping four vertebrae. Six months later, to the surprise only of those unaware of his history of swift recoveries, he was back at Goodwood, racing his red OSCA in his pale blue overalls and white helmet, drifting through Madgwick as though nothing had happened.

The following summer, during practice for the historic-car race at Le Mans, he was lapping in his Porsche when he suddenly realised that even a gentle outing in such sympathetic machinery no longer felt right. 'This afternoon I scared myself,' he admitted. 'I've always said that if I felt I wasn't up to it or that I was getting in the way of other competitors, then I'd retire. I love racing, but now's the time to stop.'

# CHAPTER 57

# POLITICALLY INCORRECT

His knighthood came in the New Year Honours list of 2000. He received it from the Prince of Wales, who remarked that it seemed long overdue. 'If it had come much earlier,' Moss replied, 'it would have been given to the wrong wife.' That drew a laugh from the Prince.

After Katie, it had taken him a while to get back into the swing. But eventually the parade resumed: the actress Judy Carne comforted him after the Goodwood crash and found herself denying rumours that they had become engaged before she jetted off to America and a career that took flight with *Rowan & Martin's Laugh-In*. Who else? Sally Ducker, Jean Clarke, Claudia Hall, Jill Stevenson, Caroline Nuttall and Sally Weston again in London. Jan Lindsey and Victoria Turner in Australia. Francesca and Albertina in Italy. Beverley and Shirlee, both air hostesses. Women called Inge, Arta and Helga. (Sally Weston, who continued to use that name, married later in the 1960s, gave birth to three children, and died of cancer in Newmarket in 1983, aged fifty-two.)

He married his second wife in 1964. Elaine Barbarino was a dark-haired, 24-year-old New Yorker who liked a good time. He flew her to London, where they were married quietly. 'It was pure sexual attraction,' he told *The Scotsman* many years later. 'She was a swinger – that is, she loved night clubs – and I didn't, so we soon had a problem.' Nevertheless, a daughter named Allison, his first child, was born on Christmas Day 1966. After four years of marriage, seeking a divorce, he commissioned a private detective who confirmed that Elaine was seeing someone else. The decree came through in 1970. Allison and her nanny spent about half the weekends of the year with him (and many years later, after her own marriage, she would give him three grandchildren). Then the parade began again until, at the third time of asking, he got lucky with Susie Paine.

His knighthood was bestowed, according to the citation, for services to motor racing. It could have added for services also to a generation of small boys, some of whom might have been inclined, as adults, to avert their gaze in 2004 when he joined the actress Joan Collins, the actor Edward Fox, the explorer Sir Ranulph Fiennes, the cricketer Geoffrey Boycott, the astronomer Sir Patrick Moore and the former Labour MP Robert Kilroy-Silk among the celebrity support- ers of the newly formed UK Independence Party.

Some of those former small boys might also have wanted to turn away from the row that erupted in 2013 after his assertion that, if they made a film of his life, he didn't want to be played by 'a poofter or anything like that'. The chap from *Skyfall* – Daniel Craig – would do, he thought. When gay rights groups reacted with outrage, he did his best to produce a measured response: 'I think it would be difficult for someone of the other persuasion, who is homosexual, to take on the part, as I have spent my life driving cars and chasing girls. I'm sorry I've caused offence, but I'm disappointed anyone could be so narrow-minded as to take offence. It was not meant to cause any. I have homosexual friends. There's nothing wrong with it. It's the way things are nowadays.'

He was from a generation that saw no need to come to terms with what was dismissively known as political correctness. Several waves of feminism had come and gone, making profound changes to society, while Moss carried on referring to 'crumpet'. Equal pay was the rule at Wimbledon and women were even welcomed into the pavilion at Lord's, but his own sport had remained largely resistant to female participation. His contemporary Maria-Teresa Di Filippis remained one of only two women to have started a Formula 1 world championship grand prix.

No one in the future will use the term 'crumpet' to describe attractive women in the way Moss continued to do until he was silenced by illness. It was a usage as patently archaic as his contemporary Tony Brooks's habit of describing a full-throttle effort behind the wheel as 'going harry-flatters'. And he was indulged. It became part of his brand. Some women – women of a certain age, perhaps, and with an ironic sense of humour – might even be amused to be described as 'crumpet'. Others would assuredly not.

The UK Independence Party was a slightly different matter. It was set up to campaign for British withdrawal from the European Union and for strengthened immigration controls. To some, this seemed an odd allegiance for a man who had seen so much of the world and who had learned how to express himself in his chosen profession on the road circuits of continental Europe, who had driven for Italian and German teams, and would presumably have appreciated the benefits of freedom of movement. But after the European elections of 2004 his name was no longer heard in connection with the political organisation through which Nigel Farage spooked David Cameron into a decision that changed the course of British history.

His early endorsement of UKIP could hardly have implied an approval of racism. When he visited South Africa for the first time, in the winter of 1959, he disliked the apartheid system on sight, and before the race in East London he advised his fellow drivers to limit their acknowledgement of the crowd to waving at the segregated enclosures reserved for non-white spectators.

The support for UKIP came from a different impulse, an affection for a certain idea of England, although in later life he claimed that he had been foolish to allow patriotism to guide so many of his decisions. 'I find it very offensive now that there is no patriotism at all,' he said. 'I was very patriotic because I loved the country. I have regrets because England now is no longer what England should be. So I certainly regret that because it was a wasted thing to do. I certainly would have been wiser not to be so patriotic. So, in hindsight, it was a mistake.'

UKIP also campaigned for lower taxation, but it might be worth noting that although a limited company was set up in 1955 to help limit Moss's tax liability, he never moved abroad to avoid paying UK tax altogether, as many other drivers would do. Some of them, such as Jim Clark, Jackie Stewart and Jenson Button, based themselves in the Bahamas or Switzerland or Monaco without a breath of criticism from the media. Not so in a more recent case, although opinions on Lewis Hamilton's tax arrangements may have been influenced by attitudes to the colour of his skin.

Moss lived to see Hamilton, a mixed-race man from a working-class family in Stevenage, be crowned champion of the world not one but six times, with a seventh still to come, often displaying a virtuosity of which he himself would have been proud, moreover securing five of those titles as only the third Englishman, after Seaman and Moss, to drive for the Mercedes Grand Prix team. In 2015, at eighty-five, Stirling joined Lewis for a gentle day out at Monza in two W196 Grand Prix cars: an open-wheeled model and the streamliner. They circulated happily for the cameras in the sixty-year-old machines, Hamilton riding high up the banking – 'We don't have that in F1 today' – while Moss stayed down low, with his memories from the season when he had followed in Fangio's wheel tracks. If he had not been entirely comfortable with the different culture – symbolised by the diamond ear studs, the braided hair, the tattoos and the friends from the world of rap music – that Hamilton brought to Formula 1, his admiration of the young champion's talent was certainly unfeigned.

# CHAPTER 58

# THE WAVE

'There was a girl with pale pink lipstick,' Moss told me in 1992, when I rang him up to say I was writing a piece about the fiftieth running of the Monaco Grand Prix and asked for his memories of a race he had won three times. 'She used to sit outside Oscar's Bar, by the side of the track going down from Casino Square to the Station hairpin. It was opposite the Metropole hotel, where I stayed every year. They gave me a twenty per cent discount. I noticed the pale pink lipstick, and I used to wave at her every time I went round.'

The Moss wave was almost as famous as the Queen's. Like Ayrton Senna's brandishing of the Brazilian national flag on a victory lap, it was something that brought him closer to the public. He made a fetish of it, and not just to celebrate a win. In the days when photographers were allowed to crouch on the grass a foot or two from the apex of a fast bend, he would spot one he knew – a Bernard Cahier, a Geoff Goddard, an Edward Eves or a Louis Klemantaski – and give an insouciant wave just as they were pressing the shutter. One man had a childhood memory of watching Moss during a practice session for a historic car meeting at Silverstone, on a day with almost no spectators at all, and noticing that he raised his hand every time he passed by. The boy looked around, wondering who it was for, before realising that it was meant for him. The wave made everyone feel good.

Once, looking back, he described it as 'just commercialisation'. As a public gesture that established his personality and enhanced his appeal, it would be noticed by race promoters, who might be prompted to offer him better starting money. It was also about getting the public involved. In front of a crowd of half a million at the Nürburgring, for example, 'if you can get a reasonable proportion of that quarter of a million waving back at you, then it's good because they're following you.' And there was never a hint of anything inauthentic about it.

Motor racing was more individual in those days. The drivers chose their own overalls. The men who ran the teams didn't feel obliged to wear the same sponsored kit as their drivers and mechanics. Neubauer had his trilby, Ugolini his Italian suits and Mays his silk shirts, handmade in Jermyn Street. Vandervell, on a hot day, had his braces on show. Even the spectators were individuals. They weren't in team livery, banding together in the grandstand like banks of football fans, in solid blocks of red or orange or blue.

No one expected a Fangio or a Moss to turn up for a press conference and parrot a line fed by a public relations manager. No one told an Uhlenhaut or an Alfieri how many cylinders they could have in their engines, or how many ratios in their gearboxes, or, for that matter, how many wheels on their cars. No one told an Alf Francis or a Guerino Bertocchi to stop working at a certain hour or took their cars away to a *parc fermé* so they couldn't do an all-nighter to fix something in time for the race. No one asked the drivers to compete on a circuit whose limits were delineated not by the natural hazards that confronted earlier generations but by colourful lines painted on asphalt.

No driver would barge a rival off the track in order to secure a championship or pre-arrange a crash in order to win a race. No one needed a system of penalty points for dangerous behaviour. No team was told they couldn't test whenever and wherever they wanted. No driver was cocooned inside a metal frame that made it even harder for the spectator to see what their hero was doing. The drivers had no mechanical devices to help them overtake a rival and no engineers coaching them through radio earpieces; once they were out there, their only guidance was what they could see, hear or feel for themselves.

But Moss was never one to bang on about how things were better in his day. In one of his early books he showed that he was looking to the future. 'The use of inter-com telephony and radar is no longer a matter of conjecture, but can practicably and practically be applied to motor racing,' he wrote in 1957 in the final paragraph of *In the Track of Speed*. 'It won't be long before we have constant contact with our pits.' When he was a guest at a modern race, he enjoyed himself. He certainly relished the skill of men like Senna, Alonso, Vettel and Hamilton. When asked, however, he would be honest. He and his generation, he felt, had enjoyed the best of it.

# CHAPTER 59

# HERO

A traffic policeman stops a speeding motorist. His first question: 'Who do you think you are, Stirling Moss?' As the decades rolled by, the name never changed. It was not 'Who do you think you are, Mike Hawthorn?' or Graham Hill or Jim Clark or John Surtees or Jackie Stewart or any of the other British drivers who actually became world champions, from James Hunt to Lewis Hamilton by way of Nigel Mansell, Damon Hill and Jenson Button. Had Moss been able to collect a royalty for every time the question was asked, he would never have needed the fees from opening BP stations or the revenue from his little property empire.

Early in his career, he became a figure whose appeal extended beyond followers of motor racing. Somehow, starting with his emergence as a teenage prodigy, he captured the imagination and the support of a wider public. Even if they had never actually seen him race, the public understood the special nature of his talent and accepted him as a symbol of his sport, just as people who wouldn't be able to tell Bach from

Beethoven knew that Yehudi Menuhin represented not just the pinnacle of violin playing but classical music at its most exalted. They also knew that in a sport where the balance between the machine and the human being often tilts in favour of the former, Moss elevated his particular skill to a kind of artistry.

His admirers could sense and share the exhilaration he experienced whenever he stepped into the cockpit, knowing that he would give it everything he had, every time. 'In all my racing career,' he told Godfrey Smith of the *Sunday Times* in 1969, 'I met a lot of fast drivers but very few fighters.' He was a fighter, whether he was in the best car in the field or the worst, or anything in between. He drove with his head but also with his heart. Some drivers, recognising that their equipment wouldn't allow them to fight at the front, settled for a respectable result. Others were known to have off days. Not Moss. 'I was always there to win,' he told Smith. Even Hawthorn once wrote of 'Stirling driving as only he can when the odds are stacked against him'.

Hawthorn had been the beneficiary of the gesture that most dramatically illustrated his rival's sense of ethics when it came to racing. Moss was not alone in believing in fairness towards his rivals: in those days, when competitors at every level were risking their lives, drivers tended to do as they would be done by, with very rare exceptions. But somehow the man in the white helmet was the one who gave the clearest impression that while he was there to win, some principles would always be more important.

His patriotism, often expressed through his desire to succeed with a British team, struck a chord with those who had watched France, Italy and Germany dominate racing between the wars and yearned for the arrival of a proper challenge. In pursuit of that objective, he sometimes chased lost causes, passing up the chance of a seat in a works Ferrari – and the certain victories it would bring – in favour of the BRM, the HWM, the ERA and the Cooper-Alta, some of which were almost comically hopeless. His bad luck – the jinxes, the gremlins, the hoodoos – became proverbial: although some accused him of bringing it on himself, through quixotic choices or harsh driving, most accepted it as a side effect of his extraordinary talent and ambition.

The admiration of his competitive spirit and willingness to fight against the odds was reinforced by the general perception of his essential seriousness of purpose. His lifestyle may in many respects have resembled that of the archetypal 1950s playboy, criss-crossing the world in permanent pursuit of what he called 'crumpet', but his true priorities were defined clearly and early. He worked hard to develop and refine his natural talent to its optimum level from every perspective – recognising, for example, that skill would have to be backed up by stamina.

He worked with almost equal diligence at the job of presenting himself to the world via the mass media. On the track, the famous wave was one means of establishing contact with the public. Throughout his life he would show no reluctance to talk to reporters, always ready with a pithy and sometimes pungent opinion, always happy to give a gossip columnist a denial of the latest rumour of an engagement to one of the pretty young actresses and models with whom he was constantly photographed. For a celebrity, he was unusually accessible. His home number was in the phone book; if you called, it would often be Moss himself, rather than his PA, who picked it up. He was happy to invite magazine journalists and TV crews into his Mayfair home, which he'd designed himself and filled with all kinds of automated devices. He road-tested cars for national newspapers and for glossy magazines. He was also much in demand for advertising campaigns: a generation of account executives had realised that this was someone to whom the public responded with warmth as well as admiration. If motor racing symbolised the speed and glamour of the modern world, he had turned himself into its embodiment.

His approach to life as a public figure was pragmatic, but never cynical. He was good company, never pompous or self-important, always alive to the world around him and interested in what others had to say. He loved telling stories or, after the big accident in 1962 blurred parts of his memory, being reminded of them. He understood how much strangers loved the chance to hear the old stories directly from his mouth, and he respected their pleasure. Even when he was being paid to attend a function – paid, in effect, for being Stirling Moss for a couple of hours – he gave the impression, without overdoing it, that there was nowhere he would rather be. To sit next to him on such an occasion was to be made to feel that there was nowhere you'd rather be, either. He also had a sense of humour extending to self-mockery: on *Desert Island Discs*, the prematurely balding 26-year-old's choice of luxury item was a bottle of hair restorer.

In 2018 his son, Elliot, told the world of his father's retirement from public life. There would be no more appearances of any sort. The announcement had mentioned his slow recovery from a recent illness. It did not say that he had been confined to bed, in and out of consciousness, for more than a year, since falling ill in Singapore.

He died peacefully at home in London on 12 April 2020 – Easter Sunday, on the bank holiday weekend that had always meant motor racing in Britain, whether bathed in sunshine or battered by hailstorm (sometimes both on the same day).

Coming a month after Britain had gone into lockdown to protect itself against the Covid-19 pandemic and newspaper obituary editors were bracing themselves for a busy time, his death received the kind of coverage due to a figure with a unique standing in the life of the nation, however remote his deeds may have seemed to the younger generations watching the black-and-white clips accompanying the TV eulogies. A private family funeral was held at Mortlake Crematorium in west London. Had it been possible in the following weeks, a memorial service would have filled St Paul's Cathedral or Westminster Abbey.

Leading a parade of her husband's cars, Lady Moss waves to the Goodwood crowd from the cockpit of an Aston Martin DBR1 (Glen Smale/Virtual Motorpix).

# CHAPTER 60

# LAP OF HONOUR

One of his first big wins had come on Easter Monday in 1949 at Goodwood, when he was still in his teens, and on Easter Monday thirteen years later his career had ended at the same circuit. It was at Goodwood during the long final illness, seven months before his death, that a tribute was mounted as part of the annual Revival meeting, in the form of a parade of his old cars. They included the Cooper-JAP in which, on the day after his nineteenth birthday, he had won a Formula 3 race at the circuit's inaugural meeting, the Vanwall which had taken him to within a point of the world championship, the Lotus 18 that had twice triumphed at Monaco, and one of the Ferrari 250GTs with which he had twice won the TT at the West Sussex track.

Leading the small flotilla was an Aston Martin DBR1, another double TT winner at Goodwood, a car with which he had proved supreme in sports car racing in the late '50s. At the wheel of the pale green car was the Duke of Richmond, the circuit's owner, whose grandfather had opened the old aerodrome to racing in 1948. In the passenger seat was Lady Moss.

Improbably enough, Stirling and Susie Paine had first met when he was thirty and she, one of two daughters of a friend in Hong Kong, was five. That was in 1959, during a stopover on his way to Australia. Later he stayed with the family on several occasions; once they had moved to London, he kept in touch. He would take Susie to dinner and she would go with him to his various rental properties, helping to clean the common parts of the buildings while he emptied the meters. They were married in April 1980, with a reception at Crockford's Club; their son arrived a few months later. For almost forty years they were inseparable, forming the strongest partnership of his life: travelling the world together, sharing the business and the privileges and the enjoyment of being Sir Stirling and Lady Moss, happy to accept the responsibility of being the centre of attention at countless events of many kinds. After the illness hit him, she could not be persuaded to leave his side. This day in West Sussex, at the scene of so many of his triumphs, was an exception.

Now here she was, wearing a black and white polka-dot frock, her blonde hair pinned back, her lipstick pink, the late-summer sun on her face, the epitome of a not-quite-bygone kind of elegance, hearing the cheers from spectators who rose to their feet as the Aston passed by and raising her hand in acknowledgment. Waving to them. Waving for him.

# ACKNOWLEDGEMENTS

The first biography of Stirling Moss was published in 1953, when he was twenty-three years old and had yet to score his first world championship point. Since then many volumes have chronicled his career. This book, written after his death, attempts to explore the scope and nature of his remarkable fame, and to examine aspects of the character behind the public image.

I must record my gratitude to the authors who preceded me, in particular the late Ken Purdy, Doug Nye, the late Alan Henry, Robert Edwards, Simon Taylor and Philip Porter, all of whom worked from a basis of undisguised admiration and in whose books can be found the fine detail of Moss's achievements. Edwards' *Authorised Biography*, for example, contains a complete race-by-race listing from 1947 to 1962.

A particular debt is also due to the late Denis Jenkinson, whose reports of Moss's feats in the pages of *Motor Sport* helped activate a schoolboy's imagination. Valerie Pirie's memoir of her association with Moss brought another and less public side of the man into view. Moss himself did historians – past, present and future – a service by keeping diaries and filling scrapbooks which are now in the possession of the Royal Automobile Club.

Clare Alexander, my agent, once again provided encouragement, as did Ian Marshall at Simon & Schuster, where Frances Jessop steered the book through the editing and production process. Adam Ferrington read the manuscript, making shrewd and helpful observations. All opinions and any residual errors are, of course, entirely my own.

# BIBLIOGRAPHY

Brooks, Tony, *Poetry in Motion* (Motor Racing Publications, 2012)

Burnside, Tom, and Denise McCluggage, *American Racing* (Könemann, 1996)

Cooper, Michael, *Sixties Motor Racing* (Palawan Press, 2000)

Cooper-Evans, Michael, *Rob Walker* (Hazleton, 1993)

Donaldson, Gerald, *Fangio* (Virgin Books, 2003)

Edwards, Robert, *Managing a Legend* (Haynes, 1997)

——, *Stirling Moss: The Authorised Biography* (Cassell, 2001)

Fangio, Juan Manuel with Roberto Carozzo, *My Racing Life* (Patrick Stephens, 1990)

Ferrari, Enzo, *My Terrible Joys* (Hamish Hamilton, 1965)

——, *Una vita per l'automobile* (Conti Editore, 1998)

Hawthorn, Mike, *Challenge Me the Race* (William Kimber, 1958)

——, *Champion Year* (William Kimber, 1959)

Hilton, Christopher, *Le Mans '55* (Breedon Books, 2004)

Jenkinson, Denis, *The Racing Driver* (Batsford, 1958)

——, *Maserati 250F* (Macmillan, 1975)

——, and Cyril Posthumus, *Vanwall* (Patrick Stephens, 1975)

Kahn, Mark, *Death Race Le Mans 1955* (Barrie & Jenkins, 1976)

Lewis, Peter, *Alf Francis: Racing Mechanic* (Foulis, 1957)

McDonough, Ed, *Vanwall: Green for Glory* (Crowood Press, 2003)

McKinney, David, *Maserati 250F* (Crowood Press, 2003)

Manso, Peter, *Vrooom!! Conversations with the Grand Prix Champions* (Pitman, 1970)

Moss, Stirling, *In the Track of Speed* (Frederick Muller, 1957)

——, with Wayne Mineau, *Book of Motor Sport* (Cassell, 1955)

——, with Maxwell Boyd, *Second Book of Motor Sport* (Cassell, 1958)

——, *A Turn at the Wheel* (William Kimber, 1961)

——, and Ken Purdy, *All But My Life* (William Kimber, 1963)

——, with Doug Nye, *All My Cars* (Patrick Stephens, 1987)

——, and Philip Porter: *Stirling Moss Scrapbooks 1929–1954, 1955, 1956–60, 1961* (Porter Press, 2005–9)

——, with Alan Henry, *All My Races* (Haynes, 2009)

——, with Simon Taylor, *My Racing Life* (Evro, 2015)

Nixon, Chris, *Mon Ami Mate: The Bright Brief Lives of Mike Hawthorn and Peter Collins* (Transport Bookman, 1991)

O'Neil, Terry, *The Bahamas Speed Weeks* (Dalton Watson, 2013)

Pirie, Valerie, *Ciao, Stirling* (Biteback, 2019)

Porter, Philip, *Stirling Moss: The Definitive Biography*, Vol. 1 (Porter Press, 2016)

Taylor, Simon, *John, George and the HWMs* (Evro, 2019)

# INDEX

Page references in *italics* indicate images.
SM indicates Stirling Moss.